THE SONG
OF ROLAND

Translated, with an Introduction by
PATRICIA TERRY
Second Edition

THE LIBRARY OF LIBERAL ARTS

published by

Macmillan Publishing Company
New York

Maxwell Macmillan Canada
Toronto

Maxwell Macmillan International
New York   Oxford   Singapore   Sydney

Editors: Maggie Barbieri and Patrick Shriner
Production Supervisor: Katherine Evancie
Production Manager: Muriel Underwood
Text Designer: Jane Edelstein
This book was set in ITC Garamond Book by V & M Graphics, Inc., and
was printed and bound by Arcata Graphics/Fairfield. The cover was
printed by Phillips Offset.

Macmillan Publishing Company
866 Third Avenue, New York, New York 10022

Macmillan Publishing Company is part of
the Maxwell Communication Group of Companies.

Maxwell Macmillan Canada, Inc.
1200 Eglinton Avenue East
Suite 200
Don Mills, Ontario M3C 3N1

Library of Congress Cataloging-in-Publication Data

The Song of Roland / translated, with an introduction by Patricia Terry.—2nd ed.
    p.   cm. — (The Library of liberal art)
  Includes bibliographical references.
  ISBN 0-02-419835-8 (pbk.)
  1. Roland   (Legendary   character)—Romances.   I. Terry,   Patricia   Ann,
  1929-   .   II. Chanson de Roland. English.   III. Series: Library of liberal art
  (Macmillan Publishing Company)
PQ1521.E5T4   1992
841'.1—dc20   91-39337
                 CIP

Printing: 2 3 4 5 6 7   Year: 4 5 6 7 8

For Nicolas, my son and Robert's,
with love for him and joy in his work

1. Marsile's Council   1-7
2. Charles' Council   8-27.
3. Ganelon + Blancandrin ride to Marsile   28-30.
4. Marsile's Council

65-135
135-186

CONTENTS

INTRODUCTION

The goals and values of literary heroes were transformed when epic gave way to courtly romance. The knight of Arthur's court, riding through the forest in quest of adventure, defending ladies under attack from gigantic aggressors, seems to reject the hero born to die on a battlefield. Yet creators of these same knights, when they wanted to claim for them an absolute courage, would say they were "like Roland." Medieval romance, as opposed to epic, was primarily concerned with individuals and their relationships. Sir Gawain was King Arthur's beloved nephew, Lancelot and Galehaut had a very impressive friendship. But the mutual fidelity of Roland and Charlemagne set a definitive standard, and the friendship of Roland and Oliver is proverbial even now.

Still, most readers of *The Song of Roland* in modern times have believed that Roland's arrogance was responsible for the unnecessary deaths of the twenty thousand men under his command. His subsequent fame, when one might have expected opprobrium, is normally explained by a contrition that the text supports very poorly. Even if it is possible to find a more satisfactory explanation for the fact that Roland alone, of all those who died at Roncevaux, is accompanied straight to God by a flight of angels, one may well question the value of a book that seems to glorify absolute monarchy, war, and religious extremism; a book that blatantly says, "Pagans are wrong; Christians are right."

Whatever it is thought to be "about," *The Song of Roland* continues to occupy a place of honor. If the reader is drawn to the poem, its perceived subject is understood in a way that seems to justify admiration. Harold March's introduction to the 1965 edition of my translation gave an interpretation that coincided with my own at that time. These pages will suggest a significantly different reading. Nevertheless, the intrinsic value of the poem remains unchanged as I perceive it. This may recommend *The Song of Roland* as an opportunity to explore the nature and contribution of a "literary masterpiece," something that can no longer be taken for granted.

It is said that when William the Conqueror was about to make the date 1066 uniquely memorable, a minstrel roused the courage of his army with a song that told of Roland. That had to be a story already familiar, and already much transformed from its historical source. The event to which the song referred totally lacks heroic grandeur. Two centuries before the Battle of Hastings, Charles, not yet Emperor or "The Great," thirty-seven years old with a moustache instead of a flowing white beard, led an expedition into Spain. Had things gone as planned, a region including Barcelona and Saragossa would have come under Frankish rule. But the first target, Saragossa, resisted, and Charles returned to France. In the Pyrenees, the baggage train and rear guard of his army were lost to treacherous local Christians. Eginhard, Charles' biographer, states that one "Hruodlandus," prefect of occupied Brittany, was killed.

Perhaps it was felt that the Emperor's reign should not be marred by inglorious defeats. T. Atkinson Jenkins points out that chroniclers had very soon augmented the scope of the battle, changed the perfidious Christians to Saracens, and held the sun still in the sky as a sign of God's favor. By the late eleventh century, the probable date of *The Song of Roland*, the time of the First Crusade, Charles' expedition to Spain could well have become exemplary, even holy.

The story, as related in the poem, tells us that after a crusade of seven years in Spain, the Franks receive a proposal of peace from Marsile, the last pagan King. They accept, although they know that Marsile cannot be trusted, because they are tired of fighting. Only Count Roland urges them to remain faithful to their cause. Roland's stepfather, Ganelon, becomes the envoy to Marsile, and plots with the pagans to destroy Roland, whom he names to command the rear guard. The Saracens attack, and although their numbers are overwhelmingly superior, they all flee or are killed. But all the Franks have been killed as well. Roland, who refused to ask Charlemagne for help at the beginning of the battle, summons him at the end. The Emperor returns to avenge the rear guard and to bring his crusade to a totally victorious conclusion.

Of the various versions extant of *The Song of Roland*, the twelfth-century Oxford Manuscript, translated here, is the oldest and the best. The manuscript is the copy of a version of the poem that was not the archetype. The poet may be the "Turoldus" mentioned in the final lines, or Turoldus may simply have been the scribe. The characters, with the possible exception of Baligant, would have already been established, although the poet perhaps invented some of the relationships among them.

The Oxford Manuscript may be merely a kind of script for an oral presentation of the poem, one moment in a continuum of changing recitations, versions noted down to be sung. But what we have before us, in itself, exists as a written work. Editors may feel entitled to make changes when another manuscript offers a way out of incoherence or a more convincing order, but such emendations are a form of respectful reading; they attempt only to restore.

The demands we make of written literature are the most stringent we can apply. Apparent faults or weaknesses are not explained away by haste or the need to recite long passages from memory. However the Oxford Manuscript came to exist, it endlessly rewards the most exigent reading. In the words of Frederick Goldin, "If we make the same demands of this poem that we would make of a written text, it responds with amazing beauty."[1]

According to Aristotle, an epic should be both complex and unified, and it has been customary, even obligatory, to respond

---

[1] Goldin, Frederick, *The Song of Roland* (New York, W. W. Norton and Company, 1978) p. 34.

to this statement by invoking Charles, rather than Roland, as the unifying figure in *The Song of Roland*. This is easy enough to defend. The poem begins and ends with the Emperor, and he is present throughout, in the thoughts and in the war cries of Roland and his men, in the fears of the Saracens. He is a majestic figure, larger than life: "No stranger needs to have him pointed out." God sends an angel to speak to him; he has prophetic dreams that show him the future, although never clearly enough for him to act on what he knows. Charles' sense of being without effective power where it matters to him most makes him human. And it builds into the poem a respect for what is given, given by God.

Roland will be unaware that the heavens grieve because he is soon to die; for Charles, God works miracles openly. The Emperor's worldly authority is sanctified by the divine. Thus his vision, however partial and dependent, dominates the poem, and it should be instructive to our reading. When Charles sees the dead at Roncevaux, he grieves that he was not there at the start of the battle; it seems not to occur to him that Roland could, or should, have called for help in time. Yet so crucial to Charles is his nephew's death that it nearly costs him his confidence in himself and in his mission, just as the true scope of that mission is being revealed. Roland's defeat of King Marsile brings a much larger figure into the field—Baligant, pagan evil incarnate. And Charles, summoned by Roland, is there to meet him. Even beyond the death of Baligant, Charles must continue to fight the Enemy, beyond the borders of this poem. But few readers will want to follow him. We call the poem *The Song of Roland* (a name that does not occur in the manuscript) because it is with Roland that we identify, regardless of our religious, political, or ethical considerations. It is not only that Roland is charismatic. It is because he alone shows us what we might not even want to see: that purity of faith, absolute belief in God, is both simple and totally ruthless.

Holy War, the war of Good against Evil, has neither beginning nor end, but we enter the poem at a point where there is a chance of making an end to one particular unfinished war. The

Emperor is camped with his army at the bottom of a hill on whose summit is Saragossa, the only unconquered pagan citadel. From the pagan King comes a message: he will follow Charles back to France, and there submit to Christianity. The reader has heard the pagans plotting this strategy; the Franks have not. Their failure to climb the hill and conquer Saragossa will be redeemed by Roland's ascent beyond Spain to heaven.

The organization of Marsile's kingdom, with its Twelve Peers, its councils, its Holy Book, looks much like that of Charles' kingdom, and yet it is also chaos. The pagans, like the Franks, love their country and will sacrifice even their sons so as not to lose her. Our ambivalence about this makes us uneasy. The deliberate sacrifice of hostages is dishonorable, quite different from freely accepted death in battle, and yet without hostages the Franks could not have believed Marsile's offer of peace. We will learn that Marsile and the Franks are not meeting for the first time. There has been a previous envoy from Marsile, and ambassadors were sent by the Franks to his court, where they were killed.

Charles' first response to the offer of peace is noncommital: it is not too late for Marsile to find salvation, but "I don't know what is in his heart." Roland says, "No good comes from Marsile!" (*Ja mar crerez Marsilie!*) English has no intensifier as emphatic as *ja*, nor a single word for *mar* meaning that evil will be the result of the action named, here believing Marsile. This is not what tired men, eager to call their task finished, want to hear. No doubt they would have accepted it from Charles, and then the war *would* quickly have been over, the Saracens of Spain converted or killed. But Roland is young, and he reinforces his argument with his credentials. He has been a great military commander, and on the strength of his commitment and contributions, he urges the Franks not to abandon their crusade.

The poet causes Roland to speak the truth, but in a tone that gets in the way of his argument. There is abundant proof that the Franks, including the Emperor, did not, in their hearts, believe Marsile. Charles would not allow any of the Peers to travel to the pagan court. This leads to the nominating of Ganelon. Whatever Roland's personal feelings—and they have been variously interpreted—Ganelon would seem a natural choice, once the Peers are all excluded. In addition, Ganelon accused Roland of pride and recklessness in wanting to refuse Marsile's offer. Logically, then, Ganelon should not be unwilling to be the ambassador. Roland, although he knew Marsile was lying, is quick to say that he himself will go. When Ganelon lets the glove, the token of his embassy, fall to the ground, everyone recognizes this as an expression of fear and a portent. This is one of several moments when the Emperor could still have intervened; instead he sends Ganelon on his way. Here is the true beginning of the Battle of Roncevaux, a failure Charles, rather than Roland, could bitterly regret. Once Ganelon makes his pact with Marsile and names Roland to the rear guard, it will not be in Charles' power to change anything.

Ganelon is not one of the Twelve Peers, the inner circle closest to the Emperor. Yet he is distinguished enough to have married the Emperor's sister, Roland's mother. These circumstances would amply explain Ganelon's resentment of Roland. Later the poet adds another motive: at his trial, Ganelon will say that because of Roland he "lost both goods and gold." Before he leaves for Marsile's court, Ganelon publicly challenges Roland and the Peers, and in all his dealings with the pagans he carefully separates Roland from Charlemagne. Thierry will argue that to harm a man in Charles' service harms the Emperor as well.

It is possible that Ganelon is sincere in his self-defence. The poet has made him eloquent, and for all the praise of Charles that fills the poem, it is Ganelon who speaks of him most impressively. To Marsile he says,

> "By God's grace, honor   illuminates my lord:
> He'd rather die   than break faith with his court."

The most astute readers have been unable to distinguish Ganelon's truth from his lies. We are, however, given a clear demonstration of his manipulation of reality when he appears before Marsile. Ganelon's account of the letter he carries from Charlemagne is quite different from the letter itself. The fictional version intends to focus Marsile's attention and emotions on Roland. The excellent idea the letter actually contains, that the Caliph be among the hostages, will be defused by an elaborate story of flight and shipwreck when Ganelon returns to the Franks. This was so convincing that a scribe, copying the text, substituted "Marganice" for "the Caliph" when the latter reappeared.

Two of Ganelon's stories are left unverified. They may, of course, refer to a lost tradition. We do not know whether Roland actually gave Charles an apple representing "the crowns of all the kings," although the language of the phrase is more like Ganelon's. The "goods and gold" may never have existed. When we question the truth of Ganelon's statements, we may forget that they are already fictions within a fiction; Turoldus, as storyteller, can seem very modern.

Pagans and Christians alike admire Ganelon's elegance and his courage; both have a negative side. His love of material wealth prompts Marsile to give him such gifts as to arouse the Franks' suspicions. His courage is tainted with bravado, as when he unnecessarily taunts Marsile, and can even prove suicidal in the service of his obsession. To remain, as he necessarily must, with Charles' army, when, sooner or later, his treachery will be found out, requires a strength of purpose close to madness. There comes a moment when the unmistakable sound of Roland's horn is heard, calling to Charlemagne. Ganelon, with astonishing self-possession, says "Just for a rabbit, he'll blow his horn all day!"

Ganelon's complexity makes more apparent the extreme simplicity, the single-mindedness, of Roland. When Ganelon's plot has come to fruition and Oliver tells Roland that Saracens are about to attack the rear guard, Roland reacts instantly, "God grant that you be right!" (*E Deus la nus otreit!*[2]) This is really

---

[2] Roland's immediate response to Marsile's peace proposal—"No good comes of Marsile!"—has the same energetic conviction.

his *only* response, and the more Oliver tries to make him understand the odds, the more Roland refuses to call for help.

The friendship of Roland and Oliver predates the Oxford Manuscript, but we do not know what made it legendary, or when Oliver entered the story. There is no Oliver in Einhard's account of Charlemagne's defeat. Brothers are named Roland and Oliver in documents from the beginning of the eleventh century.[3]

In the Oxford Manuscript, Oliver is as perfect a warrior as Roland, although he always takes second place to his companion-in-arms. His temperament is very different. Oliver argues the impossibility of fighting the immense Saracen army; for Roland what is impossible is to refuse the service of God.[4] It is God who will grant the battle; it is a gift. To alter its conditions would be a lack of faith; that is what Roland means by dishonor.[5] What some readers have thought his most egocentric moment can also be understood as absolute selflessness.[6] The purposes of God at Roncevaux are not manifested to Roland in visions or angelic communications, but in the actual circum-

---

[3] Brault, Gerard J., *The Song of Roland, an analytical edition,* vol. 1. (University Park and London, Pennsylvania State University Press, 1978), p. 4.

[4] Brault expresses this very succinctly: "To fail to grasp that, to Roland's way of thinking, *mun los*, family, France, and Emperor are the equivalent of Christianity, is to miss the entire point of *The Song of Roland,*" p. 184.

Objecting to Bédier's idea that the poem's central theme is the unresolved opposition between Roland's view and Oliver's, Brault states: "Roland experiences neither embarrassment nor guilt. Were he to speak bluntly, he would tell his friend what Christ said to Peter when the latter remonstrated with him for announcing his imminent death: "Get thee behind me, Satan! You are an obstacle in my path, because the way you think is not God's way but man's," p. 411, note 5.

I disagree with Brault's making the surface of the poem consciously, even self-consciously, Christian, although Christian attitudes certainly underlie it. Roland, in my view, would be *incapable* of speaking so "bluntly," not out of courtesy but because such a comparison would never have entered his mind, and accusations of pride would be more than appropriate if it had.

[5] In a similar spirit, Charles will say to his army, seeing the great forces of Baligant, "What does it matter how many they may be?" (3339) And the French echo him: "God sent us here to have this good cause tried!" (3368)

[6] From a different point of view, Brault identifies Roland's apparent pride as Humilitas, p. 97.

es, Turpin and Roland are still alive. The battle of
ux is a judicial combat: right will prevail against any
are reminded of this at the very end of the book when
cally unimpressive Thierry opposes the mighty Pinabel
that Ganelon is a traitor. Pinabel falls, and the Franks,
sultingly, shout, "A holy miracle!"

only sixty of the Franks are left, Roland tells Oliver
ill sound the Oliphant. He expresses grief for the loss
any valiant men, wishes that Charles were present,
n to know what has happened. Oliver, enraged, strikes
om a world they have lost forever, a world in which
vould have married Oliver's sister. In the shock of
nd suddenly realizes the vast distance between them,
ll does not understand: "You're angry with me. Why?"
omewhat pompously, explains, accusing Roland of
recklessness—the same terms Ganelon used to dis-
and's statement about Marsile. Roland makes no reply.
r, quoted approvingly by Jenkins, this silence is the
moment of the poem. Both critics understand it to
Roland's self-confidence has turned to remorse. But
is simply that Roland can give no answer that would
ngful to his friend. Archbishop Turpin does not
oland, as Jenkins states, but only complains of their
itself. No one in the poem, except Oliver, ever
s Roland for Roncevaux.

had volunteered to be part of the rear guard, and far
icting himself to ecclesiastical duties, he is one of the
ble warriors. He reminds the doomed Franks that they
martyrs.

We cannot hope   to live beyond today.
But this I tell you   is true without a doubt:
For you stand open   the gates of Paradise!

rles learns what has happened, he will avenge them
them Christian burial. Neither the Archbishop nor
uld have believed there was any possibility of rescue.

stances, which he welcomes w
Anything less, any qualification
been as if Abraham had tried to

Just as he had no need to weig
peace, Roland is totally clear-sig
as prompted by a completely in
a faith that is identical with h
never tries to explain; it is on
words where they might have b
supreme warrior, Arjuna, in *Th*
has shown him war in its abs
tatis, beyond space and time a
tions. Before Krishna's interver
ableness is not unlike Oliver'
seems useless, unnecessary des
since he will be required to k
his family. Oliver grieves for
including himself. The confro
viewpoints takes place, in bot
Krishna says to Arjuna:

Conquer yo
and fulfill y
They are a
killed by m
Be just an
the archer

Roland's assumption that al
fight for God underlies his rep
has seen from the hilltop will
weening pride or even lack
fact. Marsile's entire first arr
destroyed by twenty thousar

army fle
Roncevat
odds. W
the phys
to prove
almost ir

When
that he v
of so m
wants hir
at him fr
Roland v
this, Rola
but he st
Oliver, s
folly and
credit Ro
For Bédie
supreme
mean tha
perhaps i
be mean
reprove I
argument
reproache

Turpin
from rest
most nota
will die as

When Ch
and give
Roland co

[7] Miller, Barbara Stoler, tr., *The B*
1986), p. 104.

The effort required for the horn call to carry over such a distance, will, by the grace of the poet, cost Roland his life. No pagan is to claim that victory.

As Charlemagne and his army gallop toward Roncevaux, Roland looks about him at the dead, those who used to call him their protector. Roland has failed the trust of his men in terms of their life in the world; he offered them, instead, the eternal protection of God. His choice was made without deliberation; there was no alternative, and never would be. But now he can fully measure the price in terms of human suffering—the cause of Oliver's reproaches. In this *laisse* the absolute realm of God and the relative human world come together. Roland's men have followed him willingly and without question. They have died because he saw for them and for himself only one course of action: to fight, whatever the circumstances, for what is right.

Roland was never looking for martyrdom. Had his advice been followed when Marsile pretended submission to Charles, the purpose of the crusade would have been achieved with no significant loss to the Christian side. Now he cannot both lead his men and protect them.

This is the grief he knows he cannot survive. His saying so has been thought by many readers to indicate remorse. Harold March, quoting this *laisse*, wrote that Roland surrendered "his pride by which he caused the death of the flower of Charlemagne's army." In other words, Roland had been wrong not to try to improve the odds in the battle. This view no longer seems to me convincing. It suggests that, given another chance, Roland would have listened to Oliver's reason, would have given a rational answer to what he understood to be a religious question. How could a "good song," the very poem we are reading, be made of such an impropriety?

Roland returns to the battle, where soon Oliver calls to him, ashen, dying. Roland's certainty falters only here: "I don't know what to do," he says, and he rides on, unconscious, until he is aroused by a blow from Oliver's sword. For an instant he believes that his friend could have struck him knowingly. Oliver replies, "I recognize your voice. But I can't see you;

God keep you in His sight!" His words, intentionally or not, express their situation perfectly. "So, with great love, they parted in the end."

Oliver dies a heroic warrior's death, praying to God to bless Roland "above all other men." The Archbishop and Roland are the last alive on the field; the pagans have fled. Turpin blesses the dead before he dies of his many wounds, praying to God. Roland kills a last Saracen who would have stolen his sword, Durendal, and then he is alone, alone to carry out the majestic ceremonial of his death. Moving beyond the battlefield, further into Spain and up a hill, fainting from exhaustion and loss of blood, Roland tries in vain to destroy his sword, to keep it from pagan hands. He uses his last strength in a thrice-repeated effort; we hear the harsh grating of steel on stone, as the life of Durendal, gift of an angel to Charles, and the conquests Roland achieved for Charles with the sword, are celebrated. Then, arranging himself so that Charles will see that he "conquered until he died," Roland asks forgiveness for his sins and offers his glove to God.

Pur ses pecchez Deu puroffrid lo guant. The glove, which is throughout the poem a symbol of worldly authority, is offered to God in a spirit of penitence. Roland's last thoughts evoke all he most valued, including his military conquests. His last words express his imperfections. His authority over his life is at an end; he hands it over to God.[8] Earlier in the poem, the dropping of a glove signified fear and the presence of evil. Roland's glove, a link between him and God, does not fall, because his offering is *accepted.*

The great value of the *laisses similaires*, stanzas that suspend and repeat part of the episode, can be seen particularly well in this passage. Roland extends his glove only once, as only once

---

[8] Pauphilet calls this gesture "le geste le plus sublime de toute la littérature française" (the most sublime gesture in all French literature) but does not define it further. Jenkins' idea, which other critics have shared—that God replaced Charles as Roland's overlord—seems untenable in the light of recent research resumed in Brault's commentary, pp. 255-260, and in light of his own view of sin as a debt that must be repaid.

he places himself under the pine tree. But we are given time—
or rather, the moment is taken out of time—so that we can
experience, with increasing intensity, its extraordinary quality.
In the first *laisse* Roland offers the glove to God; in the second
laisse the right glove *has been offered* and a flight of angels
appears. There is still time for Roland to think of France, of the
Franks who followed him, of Charles, and to pray to God. Saint
Gabriel takes the glove from Roland's hand; Roland arranges his
hands in an attitude of prayer, and then he dies. One can never
sufficiently admire the daring and the discretion of this poet, the
eloquence of what he does not completely say in his words.

It is again Saint Gabriel who watches over Charlemagne's
exhausted sleep when the pagans have all been killed and he
is returning to Roncevaux. The angel sends him a vision of a
lion against whom he fights; the issue is left in doubt. The fight
against Marsile will become the much larger war with Baligant,
and finally the two leaders come face to face. Where the dream-
vision ended, Baligant, in the reality of the combat, strikes the
emperor such a blow that he staggers and nearly falls. The
advantage is with the Emir when Saint Gabriel reappears, this
time not in a dream. The words he speaks are marvelously chosen: *Reis magnes, que fais tu?*, literally, "Great King, what are
you doing?" The supernatural figure intervenes only with the
suggestion that God is impatient for Charles to triumph. Then,
restored to himself, the Emperor wields "the sword of France."

The pagans resemble the Christians; their world has a similar
structure, and they too wish for peace. They are "wrong," but
the poet has made them humanly impressive. The Franks' admiring cries—"If he were Christian, he'd be a noble knight"; "Oh
what a warrior, if he had been baptized!"—express this exactly.
We are made to feel sympathy, if not admiration, even for
Marsile. Roland has killed his son, cut off his right hand; the
King, mortally wounded, flees to Saragossa. When Baligant
arrives, Marsile is so weak he has to ask for help in order to sit
up straight in his bed. Making no mention of Ganelon, the King
takes full responsibility for the losses he has inflicted on his people. Baligant is a more impressively tragic figure—tragic in a way

impossible for those on the side of God. He has no angelic coun-
selor, but only a foreign adviser whose knowledge he respects.
Baligant has just learned of the deaths of his son and brother
when Jangleu tells him that Charles will surely triumph.
Nevertheless, the Emir goes forth to do battle, dares to suggest
that Charles, the invader, become his vassal, and his final words
in life scorn Charles' offer of Christianity. We are certainly
meant to admire him[9] and to see that Charles is not more powerful or more courageous than his opponent. He is only "right."

The Crusade ends with Baligant's defeat. The rest of the poem
is concerned with restoring order. The only Saracen still alive
and not yet baptized is the Queen, Bramimonde, protected by
Charles' command. Her rage at the inadequacy of her gods had
caused her to have their idols overthrown, despoiled, hurled into
a ditch. She praised Charlemagne's courage in the presence of
her husband and Baligant. Now, a captive in France, she is given
such education in the Faith that her conversion can be sincere.

The poet's attention to Bramimonde is surprising. The world
in which women live their lives—including Roland's mother,
Ganelon's wife, in her disregarded silence—is excluded from
the bleak domain of the poem. Bramimonde herself is rebuked
for her willful intrusion. It is startling when Oliver refers to his
sister, promised to Roland; and what reader remembers her
when Roland is dying, any more than he does himself?

Yet the poet does not, as one might have expected, let Aude
fade silently from our minds. He makes of her, in fact, a true
counterpart of Roland. Charlemagne brings her the news of
Roland's death; he offers her his own son to marry instead. This
is the voice of reason, once again, and Charlemagne's offer is
truly the best he can do. But the word he uses, *eschange*, previ-
ously occurred when Charles, riding away from Spain, ex-
pressed to Duke Naimon the full intensity of his feeling about
Roland: *Deus! se jo'l pert, ja n'en avrai escange.* (God! If I

---

[9]Although Brault does not, seeing his resemblance to Charlemagne in aspect and
gesture as distortion and irony, his response to Jangleu as self-delusion, pp.
293-294, 306.

lose him, no one can take his place.) Now he offers Aude *mult esforcét eschange.* The adjective is interesting, too; the primary meaning here is "advantageous," but there is also a strong suggestion of force. For Charlemagne, the reasonable had to be enough. Aude, having no such responsibilities in the world, proves inaccessible to good sense, deflecting it by the greater force of what she might call her honor, just as Roland invoked his "honor" and his "name" at Roncevaux.

Aude, like Roland, really has no decision to make. She replies that the Emperor's words are strange, foreign—*Cist mol mei est estrange*—because what they recommend is precisely unthinkable. "The saints and angels, almighty God forbid!"—Roland used *exactly* the same words when he refused to send for Charles. It was a formulaic expression, no doubt, but the very ground of reality in the poem. For Roland, as for Aude, experience and response are identical.

We may believe that Roland's courage made him a faultless instrument of God, or that the dark side of his courage was his pride, or, with Bédier and Eugène Vinaver, that the views of Roland and Oliver remain unresolved, that valor and wisdom can never be reconciled, nor either yield to the other. Most readers today will consider no war to be holy, nor would they give the name Joyful to a sword. But when commitment is absolute, the personal needs of the self give way to what even secular language may call a divine power. What evokes such commitment will be beyond the scope of intelligence, its object beyond judgement. We do not reduce Jeanne d'Arc to her Dauphin, or Antigone to the importance of funeral rites, or evaluate a heroic intervention by the character of the person who is rescued. The views of Roland and Oliver are *not* reconciled; Oliver does not change his mind about Roncevaux. But his love for his friend prevails, beyond the domain of judgement and opinions, or the claims of "right" and "wrong." *The Song of Roland* has no message, not even that good will triumph over evil; it brings us to experience a reality in which human affairs are contained, and to which we instinctively give homage.

1066 – Norman Invasion   pig (Anglo-Saxon)
    – Battle of Hastings.   pork (French)
    – Leadership spoke French.

laisses – stanzas of varying lengths that are bound by assonance

Chanson de geste   like lays of the scops
    ↑   ↑
   song.   heroic
              deeds

The Pilgrimage of Charlemagne.

ethos–philosophy that sets standards of behavior.
  – French are right. Saracens are wrong.
  – French cause = Christian cause
  – Saracen cause = Devil's cause.
  – light vs darkness
  ⇒ holy war = jihad

High church officials often appointed by secular rulers. Church/State joined
              Feudalism

Chronicle of Charlemagne and Roland
      – for the love of Christ.

Causes of tragedy
    – Flaw
    – Fate/circumstances (Hardy)

A NOTE ON THE TRANSLATION

I hope to have suggested that *The Song of Roland* ultimately functions much like music which, in the words of George Steiner, "brings to our daily lives an immediate encounter with a logic of sense other than that of reason."[10] The poem actually was a form of music; it was sung, and the mysterious letters AOI may be all we have of a musical notation. Jenkins suggests that the letters indicate a crescendo. There is still a kind of music in the texture of the language and in its meter. Old French, with its strong accents and emphatic consonants, is closer in sound to English than to modern French, but English has to speak in a gentler voice. The poem's most important stylistic aspect is the hypnotic drumlike rhythm of its decasyllabic verse. The lines are interrupted by a caesura after the fourth or, occasionally, the sixth syllable. Groups of such lines, called *laisses*, held together by assonance, segment the driving rhythm, the ground bass, bringing into focus one facet of the drama at a time.

No matter how carefully lines of English verse may be constructed so that in syllable count and accentuation they imitate the meter of *La Chanson de Roland*, the English-speaking reader, unaccustomed to a regular caesura, habitually fails to notice it. Instead of having four principal accents in a line, the meter tends to be distorted into a vague iambic pentameter; and if the marching rhythm is lost, most of the poem's power goes with it.

The best solution I could find was simply to indicate the caesura by an actual break in the line. This creates at least a sufficiently heavy stress on the preceding syllable, if not a real pause. Although, in the old French, either segment of a line can end in an uncounted and unaccented syllable, the lines in this version all end with an accented syllable. I hoped, by this device, to compensate for the lack of assonance that, even if less effective in English than in Old French, would still have been an

---

[10]*Real Presences* (Chicago: University of Chicago Press, 1989), p. 218.

asset. Unfortunately, my attempts to reproduce it resulted in excessively complicated syntax and too many departures from the actual expressions of the text. On the other hand, I have tried to indicate that the *laisse* functions as a dramatic unit by ending each one with a strong assonance or rhyme.

Where proper names have a form familiar in English, I have used it: Marsile (not Marsilie or Marsilions), Ganelon (not Guenes, Guenles, or Guenlon); in general I have followed what seemed the simplest procedure in each case, refraining, however reluctantly, from the possibility in Old French of having two forms with differing numbers of syllables to designate a single character.

The syntax of the poem is so simple that the least departure from the techniques of plain English prose seemed in the worst sense "poetical," because the final effect of this simplicity is grandeur. The vocabulary is equally strict in its avoidance of anything in the least elaborate; the poem rejects oversophisticated words as a living organism expels a foreign body. Yet in spite of the generally flat diction, certain statements have an intensity very difficult to reproduce in translation. Often this is because the emphasis falls so perfectly on the words. After Charles has pursued the victorious pagans to their destruction, he retraces his steps, and finds himself: *En Rencesvals, la o fut la bataille.* English would have no way to achieve the balance of that line, if only because "battle" ends in an unaccented syllable. *La* (there) and *o,* (where) replicate the idea of location, as the English words also do, but with a heaviness that detracts from the strength of the nouns. *Fut* means "was," but the English auxiliary has little power without an accompanying verb of action, while the French verb is specific for events in the past, things that happened, and has a more emphatic quality. It also receives a strong accent. The line would be read: En *Rencesvals la* o *fut* la *bataille,* with heaviest accent falling on the last word. The meaning of the line can be conveyed, and something of the emotion, but not its apparently artless dramatic effect.

The appreciation of transparent art most often comes with long familiarity; lines that are deeply moving to initiates may cause newer readers to complain of impoverished description:

Halt sunt li pui e li val tenebrus,
Les roches bises, li destreiz merveillus.

To say that the hills separating France from Spain are high and the valleys dark would seem no great contribution to literature, but these lines, which become a variable refrain, make the very landscape participate in the drama. *Halt sunt li pui* suggests the aspirations of the Franks and the difficulty of realization; *tenebrus* is not just shadowy, but fear of what the shadows may conceal. In the next line, *roches* (rocks) echoes the assonance; *bise* is the only color, dark or brownish grey, and its precision puts us differently in the perspective of the viewer. *Destreit* means "a narrow passage," but also "hardship, torment." *Merveillus* means "a source of wonder," but also "terrible and terrifying." All these meanings emanate from the ordinary words. The translator will not readily achieve, in equally plain language, a similarly complex effect, and will have to choose, for every phrase, between the prosaic and too overt appeal to the reader's emotions.

Many enriching details tend to be obscured by the unemphatic style, and translation must leave these to the reader's appreciation. A few might be pointed out here. There is often a synthesis of the practical and the symbolic. Marsile, when we first see him, reclines in the shade of an orchard, partly because it is hot in the sun, partly because he less literally flees the light. His position suggests a contrast with Charles, upright on his throne. Often the poet's precision convinces us of the unlikely: Falsaron's forehead is six inches or more across, Roland's sword slashes through the spine of Chernuble's horse without looking for a joint. The affective resonance of certain words influences the action or our reaction: Blancandrin evokes *clere Espaigne la bele* (this shining land, fair Spain), for which sons will more readily be sacrificed; the faintly sententious quality of some of Oliver's remarks guarantees that our sympathies will remain with Roland. Perhaps this is analogous to the tone of Roland's first speech, which the Franks found more boastful than persuasive. Minute devices indicate emotion, as when Charlemagne strokes or twists or pulls his beard. Other details have a psychological significance: Ganelon, "who'd rather not be there," drops the glove. When Roland doesn't, the significance is transcendence.

We know essentially nothing about the poet we call Turoldus, but we do know that someone shaped the poem we call *La Chanson de Roland*, devoted to it his care and craftsmanship, and let it use resources in him beyond his own knowledge. As Brault writes, concerning the imagery of the poem, "Such figurative language could not be understood or appreciated in the same way by everyone in the audience, but, then, could carved capitals or remotely situated sculpture have been grasped—or, for that matter, even *seen*—by every individual viewing a Romanesque church? The fact that the patterns of imagery . . . may not have been consciously arrived at by the poet does not mean that they do not exist."[11] The poem that surprises us increasingly the more we know it must surely have been, for its author too, a voyage of discovery, and there is no reason to imagine that we are more sensitive than he to the beauty we encounter on our way. Readers from vastly different times and places, of totally dissimilar beliefs, have been responsive to that beauty, perhaps each in a different way; and "beauty" is something recognized rather than explained. It shines through our experience of the poem as Roland's joyful radiance illuminates our vision of Roncevaux.

Since the first publication of this translation, in 1965, there has been much new research on *The Song of Roland*, with an increased emphasis on its literary qualities rather than on the historical or philological. The work of many scholars has contributed to my understanding of the text; I am particularly indebted to Gerard J. Brault's invaluable analytical edition. There has also been the extraordinary work of Cesare Segre, whose meticulous edition of the Oxford Manuscript includes documentation on all the previous editions, and all versions of the poem through the fifteenth century. He confirms the more convincing arrangement of *laisses* 113 to 126 as it appears in certain other

[11]*The Song of Roland*, p. 57.

editions, and elucidates many difficult passages. My translation has been revised to conform to his emendations, and all quotations are from his text. Other revisions have come from changes in my way of reading the text; the influence of my students over the years, with their changing views, has been a significant factor. Some passages have been altered because my practice of translation has become more austere, trusting the text to speak more for itself.

It is always a special pleasure to acknowledge the contributions of friends: Charlotte Joko Beck's enlightening suggestions, direct and indirect; Kathleen and Tom Micklow's constant support and sensitive readings; the perceptive comments of my colleague Nancy Vine Durling; the generosity and skill of Helen Anderson, physician and friend. Catherine Lowe, experienced in the teaching of this text, persuaded me to make important clarifications. To my personal editor, Helene J. F. de Aguilar, grateful thanks; her approval carries conviction and her negative comments open rewarding perspectives. In this, as in all my work, the participation and the encouragement of my husband, his patience and his concern for my time and energy, are not to go without saying.

SOME IMPORTANT STUDIES AND EDITIONS

Auerbach, Erich. *Mimesis*. Translated by Willard Trask. Garden City, NY: Doubleday Anchor Books. 1953.

Bédier, Joseph. *La Chanson de Roland commentée*. Paris: Piazza. 1968.

————, ed. *La Chanson de Roland*. Paris: Piazza. 1937.

Brault, Gerard J. *The Song of Roland: An Analytical Edition*. 2 vols. University Park: Pennsylvania State University Press. 1978.

Calin, William C. *A Muse for Heroes: Nine Centuries of the Epic in France*. Toronto: University of Toronto Press. 1983.

————, ed. *La Chanson de Roland*. New York: Appleton-Century-Crofts. 1968.

Cook, Robert Francis. *The Sense of The Song of Roland*. Ithaca and London: Cornell University Press. 1987.

Dufournet, Jean. *Cours sur La Chanson de Roland*. Paris: Centre de Documentation universitaire. 1972.

Duggan, Joseph J. *The Song of Roland: Formulaic Style and Poetic Craft*. Berkeley and Los Angeles: University of California Press. 1973.

Faral, Edmond. *La Chanson de Roland: Etude et analyse*. Paris: Mellottée. 1934.

Goldin, Frederick, tr. *The Song of Roland*. New York: W. W. Norton. 1978.

Jenkins, T. Atkinson, ed. *La Chanson de Roland: Oxford Version*. Boston: Heath. 1924.

Jones, George F. *The Ethos of The Song of Roland*. Baltimore: Johns Hopkins University Press. 1963.

Le Gentil, Pierre. *La Chanson de Roland*. Paris: Hatier-Boivin. 1955.

Lejeune, Rita, and Jacques Stiennon. *La Légende de Roland dans l'art du moyen âge*. 2 vols. Brussels: Arcade. 1967. English translation by Christine Trollope. *The Legend of Roland in the Middle Ages*. New York: Phaidon. 1971.

Pauphilet, Albert. *Le Legs du Moyen Age: Etudes de littérature médiévale*. Melun: Librairie d'Argences. 1950.

Rychner, Jean. *La Chanson de geste*. Geneva: Droz. 1955.

Segre, Cesare, ed. *La Chanson de Roland*. 2 vols. Translated by Madeleine Tyssens. Geneva: Droz. 1989.

Vance, Eugene. *Reading The Song of Roland*. Englewood Cliffs, NJ: Prentice-Hall. 1970.

Vinaver, Eugène. *A la Recherche d'une poétique médiévale*. Paris: Librairie Nizet. 1970.

Act I   Exposition   I
Act II   Battle (Roland vs. Marsile)   II } revenge
Act III Chase   III   } revenge
Act IV   Battle (Charlemagne vs. Baligant)
Act V   Ganelon's Trial   I

Duplication — 2 battles (like 2 trolls in Beowulf)
Exposition — Roland vs. Ganelon (personal)
Battle A — French vs. Saracens (local)
Battle B — Christians vs. Pagans (universal)

THE SONG OF ROLAND

Saracens – Moors.

Act I
Scene 1

1

The mighty Charles,   our Emperor and King,
Seven long years   has been at war in Spain;
That lofty land   lies conquered to the sea.
No fortress now   is standing in his way,
No walls, no towns   remain for him to break,
Except for Saragossa,   high on its hill,
Ruled by Marsile,   who has no love for God;
He serves Apollo,   and to Mohammed prays—
But he will come,   and soon, to evil days! AOI

2

In Saragossa,   the pagan King, Marsile,   *10*
Walks through an orchard,   in the shadow of the trees.
The King reclines   on a blue marble bench;

8. The gods of the Saracens are Apollin, Mahumet, and Tervagant. The origins
of the first two are obvious, but it should be understood that as they are
conceived by the *Roland* poet the one was no more appropriate to the
Mohammedans than the other. As for Tervagan, or Tervagant, even his source is
obscure. The Saracens in the poem worship idols, and although the laws of their
gods are written down in a book, this would indicate at best a very faint aware-
ness of the Koran.

His host assembles,   some twenty thousand men.
He speaks these words   to all his dukes and counts:
MARSILE "Now hear, my lords,   what evils weigh us down!
For Charles has come,   the ruler of sweet France,
To seize our lands,   and bring us to our knees.
I have no army   to fight against his own;
No men of mine   will drive him to defeat—
20   Give me your counsel,   as you are true and wise,
Save me from death,   and from this bitter shame."
Mute are the pagans,   except for one alone:
Blancandrin speaks,   whose castle is Val-Fonde.

3

Among the pagans   Blancandrin was wise,
A trusted vassal,   a brave and loyal knight,
Clever enough   to think of good advice.
BLANCANDRIN He tells the King,   "You need not be afraid.
Send word to Charles,   the arrogant, the proud,
That you in friendship   salute him as your lord.
30   Offer him gifts: bears and lions and dogs,
And seven hundred camels,   a thousand hawks,
Four hundred mule-loads   of silver and of gold,
And fifty carts   to form a wagon-train.
He'll have enough   to pay his hired men.
He has campaigned   so long here in this land,
He won't refuse   to go back home to Aix.
Say you will meet him   in France, on Michael's Day,

---

16. The adjective is so nearly part of the noun that even the Saracens speak of *dulce France.*
24. In the *laisses similaires* that occur at several of the poem's most dramatic moments, the action is suspended while the content of a *laisse* is restated with a different assonance. The point of view is somewhat altered, and the emotion intensified.
31. Mewed (adult) hawks.
36. Aix la Chapelle.

To be converted,   adopt the Christian law,
And do him homage   in friendship and good will.
If hostages are needed,   say you will send   *40*
Ten, even twenty,   to witness your good faith:
We'll have to yield   the sons our wives have borne—
It's certain death,   but I will send my own.
Better that they   should sacrifice their heads
Than that we lose   our honor and our pride,
And live as beggars   with all our rights denied!" AOI

4

Said Blancandrin,   "I swear by my right hand,
And by this beard   that ripples on my chest,
You'll see the French   disband their troops and go,
The Franks will soon   be on their way to France.   *50*
And when each one   has found his home again,
Charles, in the chapel   that he has built in Aix,
Will give a feast   in honor of the saint,
On Michael's Day,   when we'll have sworn to come—
But of our coming   the French will see no sign.
The King is proud,   and cruel is his heart;
He'll have the heads   of all our men cut off.

43. Since the Saracens have no intention of fulfilling their promises, and consid-
ering their no doubt correct understanding of Charles (56), Blancandrin would
very likely be explicit here about the sacrifice involved. However, the expression he uses, *par num d'ocire*, is repeated in his speech to Charlemagne, where
it could not have the same meaning, or it would reveal the pagans' plan.
Goldin's "named to die" might serve both circumstances; Brault gives "though it
means certain death for him" in line 43 and "although it means risking his life" in
line 149.
50. The "Franks" (*Francs*) and "French" (*Françeis*) are for the most part used as
synonymous terms. Occasionally, however, the Franks of France are distinguished from the Franks from elsewhere in the Empire. It is stated that Charles
prefers the men of France to all others (3031); in lines 3976-77 the bishops of
France are mentioned separately from those of Bavaria and Germany. The
boundaries of "France" are also variable, sometimes including the whole of
Charlemagne's empire (larger than life), sometimes more restricted.

But better far   that they should lose their heads
Than that we lose   this shining land, fair Spain,
60   And be condemned   to hardship and disgrace."
PAGANS   The pagans say,   "That may well be the case!"

5

The King declared   the council at an end.
He summoned forth   Clarin of Balaguer,
Estramariz,   and Eudropin his peer,
Long-bearded Guarlan,   and with him Priamon,
And Machiner,   his uncle Maheu,
And Joüner,   Malbien d'Oltremer,
And Blancandrin,   to be his embassy;
These ten he chose   from his most evil men.
MARSILE 70   "Barons, my lords,   you'll go to Charlemagne;
He is in Cordres,   holding the town besieged.
The olive branch   you'll carry in your hands,
A sign of peace   and your humility.
If you are clever,   if you persuade the King,
Much gold and silver   shall be your thanks from me,
Fiefdoms and land,   as much as you desire."
PAGANS   The pagans say,   "That's all that we require." AOI

6

Then King Marsile   declares the council closed.
MARSILE   He tells his men,   "Thus you shall go, my lords:
80   Hold in your hands   the olive branch of peace,
And speak for me   to Charlemagne the King;

71. "Cordres" suggests Cordova, but that city would then be in northern Spain.
The poet's notions of geography are vague, and no more than a general effect
can be derived from them. The same applies to the names of the more exotic
peoples, especially among Baligant's pagans.

In his God's name,   ask him to grant me grace.
Say that before   a single month has passed,
I'll bring to France   a thousand of my men,
There be converted,   adopt the Christian law,
Become his vassal   In loyalty and love.
For this he'll have   what hostages he will."
PLAN Says Blancandrin,   "Our wishes he'll fulfill." AOI

7

The ten white mules   are brought for them to ride;
Suatilie's King   had sent them to Marsile.   *90*
Their bits are golden,   their saddles silver-trimmcd.
The envoys mount,   and as they ride away,
Each in his hand   holds high the olive branch.
They go to Charles,   who rules the Frankish land;
He won't see all   the treachery they've planned. AOI

Scene 2

8

The Emperor Charles   is joyful, jubilant:
The lofty walls   of Cordres are torn down,
His catapults   have laid its towers low;
His knights rejoice,   for great is their reward—
Silver and gold,   and costly gear for war.   *100*
In all the city   no pagan now remains
Who isn't dead   or one of the true Faith.
In a great orchard,   Charlemagne sits in state.
With him are Roland,   and Oliver, his friend;
A Duke called Samson,   and fiery Anseïs,
Geoffroy of Anjou,   flag-bearer for the King;
The two companions   Gerin and Gerier.

106. Geoffroy of Anjou carries the *gonfalon*, or battle flag.

And with these barons   is no small group of men,
For fifteen thousand   came with them from sweet France.
110   The knights are seated   on carpets of white silk;
The older men,   or clever, pass the time
Playing backgammon,   or else they sit at chess;
The nimble youths   prefer to fence with swords.
Beneath a pine,   beside a briar-rose,
A throne is placed—   it's made of purest gold.
There sits the King,   the ruler of sweet France;
White is his beard,   and silver streaks his hair,
Handsome his form,   his bearing very proud:
No stranger needs   to have him pointed out.
120   The Saracens dismount   and come on foot
To greet the King,   as friendly envoys would.

9

Then Blancandrin   begins to make his speech.
He says to Charles,   "May God grant you His grace,
That glorious Lord   to whom all men must pray!
We've come to you   at King Marsile's command;
He's learned about the law   that saves men's souls,
And of his wealth   he wants to offer you
Lions and bears,   and hunting dogs on chains,
And seven hundred camels,   a thousand hawks,
130   Silver and gold   four hundred mules will bear,
And fifty carts   to form a wagon-train.
These will be loaded   with silver coins and gold,
Enough for you   to well reward your men.
You have campaigned   so long here in this land,
It must be time   to go back home to Aix;
My lord Marsile   says he will follow you."
The Emperor Charles   holds both hands up toward God;
He bows his head,   and gives himself to thought. AOI

10

The Emperor Charles   sits with his head bent low.
He was not known   for answering in haste: *140*
Always he liked   to take his time to speak.
When he looked up,   his face was stern and proud.
Thus he replies: "You've spoken well indeed.
But King Marsile   has been no friend of mine;
Of what you say,   although your words are fair,
How shall I know   how much I can believe?"
"Take hostages,"   the Saracen replies,
"Ten or fifteen   or twenty you shall have;
Though he risks death,   I'll send a son of mine,
And there will be   some even nobler men.   *150*
When, in your palace   at Aix, you hold the feast
That celebrates   Saint Michael of the Sea,
My lord Marsile   declares that he will come,
And, in those baths   which were God's gift to you,
He will be baptized,   adopt the Christian faith."
Then answers Charles,   "It still is not too late." AOI

11

Beautiful was the evening,   the sun shone clear.
By Charles' command   the mules were led to stalls.

140. The shifts of tense in *Roland* sometimes seem to provide dramatic emphasis by bringing an action closer to the reader, but often have no apparent purpose. I have followed them whenever such accuracy was not obtrusive.
152. Seint Michel del Peril, elsewhere, *de la Mer del Peril*; the attribute of the sanctuary, Mont St. Michel, accessible only at low tide, was given to the saint.
154. The mineral springs and baths at Aix, or, as Jenkins suggests, the buildings connected with them in which the ceremony of baptism would take place. Their supernatural origin is not mentioned by Einhard, but many such divine contributions embellished the legend of Charlemagne.

In the great orchard   he had a tent set up,
160   And there he lodged   the envoys of Marsile;
Twelve of his servants   attended to their needs.
There they remained   until it was bright day.
When, in the morning,   the Emperor arose,
He heard a mass   and matins first of all,
And then the King   sat down beneath a pine,
And called his barons: for what he must decide
The men of France   would always be his guide. AOI

12

Beneath a pine   the Emperor takes his place,
And calls his barons   to say what they would do.
170   Duke Ogier,   Archbishop Turpin came,
Richard the Old,   his nephew called Henri,
From Gascony   the brave Count Acelin,
Thibaut of Reims,   his cousin Count Milon,
And there were both   Gerin and Gerier—
Count Roland came,   together with these two,
And Oliver,   so noble and so brave;
The Franks of France,   more than a thousand men.
Ganelon came   by whom they were betrayed.
And then began   the talks that evil swayed. AOI

13

180   "Barons, my lords,"   says Charles the Emperor,
"This I have heard   from envoys of Marsile:
Of his great wealth   he'll send me a good part,
Lions and bears,   and hunting dogs on chains,
Seven hundred camels,   a thousand hawks,

161. The word in the text is *serjanz*, usually translated as "sergeants." They apparently function, however, as personal attendants of the higher-ranking knights.

Four hundred mule-loads   of fine Arabian gold,
And with these gifts,   some fifty heavy carts.
But he requests   that I return to France,
And says that when   I'm home again in Aix,
He'll come and yield   to holy Christian law,
He'll take the Faith,   and hold his lands from me;   190
But I don't know   the secrets of his heart."
"We must think twice,"   they say, "before we start!" AOI

14

The King has brought   his discourse to an end.
And now Count Roland   has risen to his feet;
He speaks his mind   against the Saracens,
Saying to Charles,   "No good comes of Marsile!
It's seven years   since first we came to Spain;
For you I've conquered   Noples and Commibles,
I took Val-Terre   and all the land of Pine,
And Balaguer,   Tudela, Sedille.   200
There King Marsile   displayed his treachery:
Of his vile pagans   he sent to you fifteen;
Each in his hand   held high the olive branch,
And when they spoke,   we heard this very speech.
You let your Franks   decide what should be done;
The plan they chose   was foolishness indeed:
You sent two Counts   as envoys to the King,
Basant was one,   the other was Basile—
They left their heads   on a hill near Haltilies!
Finish the fight   the way it was begun: 210
To Saragossa   lead on your gathered host,
Besiege the city,   at any cost, remain;
Avenge those men   so villainously slain!" AOI

212. *A tute vostre vie.* There is no reason for the siege of Saragossa to take a lifetime, nor would the thought have been encouraging. I understand the phrase, as Brault does, to mean "give it all you have."

15

The Emperor Charles   has kept his head bowed down;
He strokes his beard,   arranges his moustache,
And to his nephew   says neither yes nor no.
The French are silent,   except for Ganelon;
He stands up straight   and comes before the King,
With wrathful pride   begins his argument,
220 Saying to Charles: "Believe no underling,
Not me, not Roland,   who speaks against your good!
When King Marsile   sends messengers to say
He'll place his hands in yours,   and be your man,
He'll do you homage   for all the lands of Spain,
And he'll observe   our holy Christian law—
Whoever urges you   to scorn this peace
Does not care, Sire,   what kind of death we die.
A man too proud   will recklessly advise;
Let's heed no fools,   and keep to what is wise!" AOI

16

230 When he had stopped,   Duke Naimon rose to speak;
Charles had no vassal   respected more than he.
He said to Charles,   "You've heard Count Ganelon;
I think the answer   that he has given you

220. Ganelon's first words, *Ja mar crerez bricun*, echo Roland's *Ja mar crerez
Marsilie!* (196), and this would seem to indicate immediately the basic motiva-
tion of his argument. Probably Ganelon does believe that Marsile's offer should
be accepted, but his main interest is in seizing the chance of effectively oppos-
ing Roland. Very likely Ganelon had not considered the possibility of being made
ambassador to Marsile, and the unpleasantness of this surprise accounts for his
violent reaction in *laisse* 20. That he was not a coward is well demonstrated
elsewhere.
   Just why Ganelon so hates Roland is not known to us, but the poet who made
Roland his stepson supplied a powerful motive.

Contains good sense,   if it be understood.
For King Marsile   there's no hope in this war:
All of his castles   have fallen to your hands,
Your catapults   have broken down his walls,
His towns are burned,   his men brought to defeat.
Now envoys ask   your mercy for the King—
If we refuse,   we're guilty of grave sin.   240
Since hostages will prove   he did not lie,
In this great war   there's no one left to fight."
The Frenchmen say,   "The Duke is in the right!"

17

"Barons, my lords,   which one of you shall go
To Saragossa,   to talk with King Marsile?"
Duke Naimon says,   "I'll do it, by your leave.
Yield to me now   the envoy's staff and glove."
"Your wisdom's needed here!"   the King replied.
"By this white beard,   by my moustache I swear
So far from me   I'll never let you go.   250
Sit down; if you are wanted,   I'll let you know!"

18

"Barons, my lords,   what envoy can we send
To Saragossa,   held by the Saracen?"

234. Jenkins understands the line to mean "provided that it [Ganelon's counsel]
be properly understood." He feels that Ganelon's meaning was obscured by his
emotions. The speech seems to me clear enough, but Naimon's restatement is
certainly more objective. Bédier's reading, "You have only to do what he says,"
seems less likely.
246. Roland has sometimes been criticized for not being the first to offer to go.
But Naimon, who approved Ganelon's speech, would have to volunteer immediately.

Count Roland says,   "Let me talk to Marsile!"
"No, you shall not!"   Count Oliver replies,
"Your heart is fierce,   and you are quick to wrath—
If you are sent,   there's sure to be a fight.
By the King's leave,   I'll be the one to go."
Answers the King,   "Be quiet, both of you!
260   Not you nor he   will set foot in that town!
And by this beard   that you can see is white,
I'll tell you now   the Twelve Peers all must stay."
The French are silent;   they dare not disobey.

19

Turpin of Reims   has risen from his place.
He says to Charles,   "Let all your Franks stay here.
For seven years   you've fought to win this land
Where they have suffered   great hardships and fatigue.
Give, Sire, to me   the envoy's staff and glove,
And I will seek   the Spanish Saracen;
270   I would be glad   to know what he is like."
But much displeased,   the Emperor replies,
"I'll hear no more—   go to your place and sit.
Keep your advice   until I ask for it!" AOI

20

"My valiant knights,"   says Charles the Emperor,
"Choose for me now   the nobleman of France
Who is to take   my message to Marsile."
"I name," says Roland,   "Stepfather Ganelon."
The Franks reply,   "He'd do it very well;
We could not make   a wiser choice than this."
280   Count Ganelon   half choking in his rage,
Pulls from his neck   the splendid marten furs,

Over a tunic   made of the finest silk.
Steel-grey his eyes   and very proud his face,
His carriage noble,   his chest is large around;
He looks so handsome,   his peers all turn and stare.
He says, "You fool,   rash are your words, and wild.
Everyone knows   I'm stepfather to you,
Yet you name me   the envoy of Marsile!
If God should grant   that I come home again,
I won't forget—   be sure I'll find a way   290
To pay you back,   as long as you're alive!"
"I hear," says Roland,   "your foolishness and pride.
Everyone knows   I answer threats with scorn;
A man of wisdom   this embassy requires—
I'll take your place,   if the King so desires." AOI

21

Ganelon says,   "You shall not take my place!
You're not my man,   nor am I your liege-lord.
King Charles commands me   to serve him in this way:
In Saragossa   I'll talk to King Marsile.
But something else,   some kind of prank I'll play,   300
Fit to relieve   my fury at this wrong."
Roland replies   with laughter loud and long. AOI

22

Count Ganelon,   when he hears Roland laugh,
Suffers such pain   he nearly splits with rage,
And he comes close   to falling in a faint.
He says to Roland,   "I have no love for you,
For you have swayed   this council to your will!
My rightful King,   you see me here at hand,
Ready to do   whatever you command." AOI

23

310   "To Saragossa   I know that I must go.
And from that journey   no man comes to his home.
Remember this: your sister is my wife;
She bore my son—   there is no fairer youth—
His name is Baldwin;   he'll make a valiant man.
To him I leave   my fiefdoms, all my lands.
Grant him your care;   I'll see him not again."
Then answers Charles,   "You have too soft a heart.
You know my will;   it's time for you to start." AOI

24

Thus spoke the King,   "Come forward, Ganelon.
320   Take now from me   the envoy's staff and glove;
You've heard the Franks,   and they have chosen you."
Says Ganelon,   "Sire, this is Roland's work;
I'll have no love,   as long as I may live,
Either for him   or Oliver his friend.
All the Twelve Peers,   to whom he is so dear,
Sire, in your presence,   I challenge here and now!"
Then says the King,   "You yield too much to wrath.
Now you shall go,   since that is my command."
"I'll have the same   protection from Marsile
330   You gave Basant   and his brother Basile." AOI

317. Charles' irritated reply seems astonishing; one wonders if it does not conceal his embarrassed unwillingness to admit, once Ganelon has, to Charles' relief, been chosen, that the mission is indeed extremely dangerous.
330. So Ganelon was, after all, impressed by the fate of Basin and Basile, although he paid no attention to it in his response to Roland's speech. It is also mentioned in Charles' letter to Marsile.

25

→ gauntlet – symbol of
  commission and
  authority to
  negotiate.

The Emperor Charles   holds out his right-hand glove,
But Ganelon,   who'd rather not be there,
Taking the gauntlet,   lets it fall to the ground.
The Frenchmen say,   "Oh, God! What does this mean?
Surely this message   will bring us to our woe.
Says Ganelon,   "Your answer won't be slow."

26

"Sire," says the Count,   "now grant me leave to go;
Since go I must,   I care not for delay."
The King replies,   "In Jesus's name and mine!"
Then Charles' right hand   absolves the Count from sin;   *340*
The staff and letter   are both given to him.

27

Count Ganelon   returning to his tent,
Arrays himself   as if for waging war
With the best arms   his household can provide.
The spurs are golden   he fastens to his feet,
Murglais, his sword,   is hanging at his side,
And now he mounts   his war-horse Tachebrun,
The stirrup held   by his uncle Guinemer.
Then you could see   how many knights shed tears,
All of them saying,   "Alas! You go to die.   *350*
Long have you served   the great King at his court,
A noble vassal;   none fail to speak your praise.
The man who named you   the envoy of Marsile

---

340. One of several examples in the poem of Charlemagne's priestly function.

Will not live long—   in spite of Charlemagne!
Roland was wrong   not to remember this:
Behind you stands   a mighty family."
And then they say,   "Let us go with you, lord."
The Count replies,   "Almighty God forbid!
I'll die alone,   not sacrifice good knights.
360   But you must go,   my lords, back to sweet France
Where you will bring   my greetings to my wife,
To Pinabel,   my good friend and my peer,
And to my son,   Baldwin, whom you all know—
Give him your help,   and serve him as your lord."
Now toward Marsile   Ganelon sets his course. AOI

Scene 3

28

Ganelon rides   under tall olive trees;
Now he has met   the envoys from Marsile.
Blancandrin waits   to ride with the French knight.
Both of them talk   with great diplomacy.
370   Says Blancandrin,   "I marvel at your King—
For he has conquered   the whole of Italy,
And then to England   he crossed the salty sea
So that the Saxons   would pay Saint Peter's fee.
And what of Spain   will Charlemagne require?"
The Count replies,   "That's hidden in his mind.
A greater King   no man will ever find." AOI

29

Says Blancandrin,   "The Franks are noble men;
But they do wrong,   those warlike dukes and counts

375. At his trial, Ganelon will insist that he was always loyal to Charlemagne.
His conversations with Blancandrin and Marsile show him punctiliously respectful to the Emperor, and often convincingly admiring: The most splendid praise
of Charles in the poem comes from Ganelon (*laisse* 40).

When by the counsel   they give to Charlemagne
They wear him out,   and others suffer too."   *380*
Ganelon says,   "Of this I could accuse
Only Count Roland—   who'll pay for it some day.
Not long ago,   when Charles sat at his ease,
His nephew came   dressed in his battle gear—
He'd gone for plunder   somewhere near Carcasonne.
In Roland's hand   an apple shone, bright red;
He told his uncle,   'Accept it, my fair lord!
I bring you here   the crowns of all the kings.'
But his great pride   will lead him on too far,
For every day   we see him risk his life.   *390*
If he were killed,   there'd be an end to strife." AOI

willing to make a deal

30

Says Blancandrin,   "Evil is Roland's heart.
He'd have the world   surrender to his will,
Proclaim his right   to every land on earth!
But by whose help   can he attempt so much?"
"The Franks of France!   He so commands their love,
They'll never fail him,   they're with him to a man.
He gives them gifts   of silver and much gold,
War-horses, mules,   brocades and costly arms;
The King himself   won't cross him in the least: *400*
By Roland's sword   he'll rule to the far East!" AOI

Scene 4.

31

So Ganelon   and Blancandrin ride on
Until they've made   a solemn pact: they vow
That they will seek   to have Count Roland slain.

---

400. This line could also mean that Roland gives the Emperor everything the latter wants, which is equally true.

They go their way,   and then dismount at last
In Saragossa   where a tall yew tree stands.
Under a pine   a throne has been set up,
Draped in brocade   of Alexandrian silk.
There sits the King,   the ruler of all Spain;
410   Around him wait   his twenty thousand men.
Not one of them   lets fall a single word;
They're all intent   on what they hope to hear
From those two men   who even now appear.

32

Now Blancandrin   has come before Marsile,
And by the fist   he holds Count Ganelon.
He speaks these words: "Mohammed keep you safe,
Apollo too,   whose Law we all obey!
We have delivered   your message to King Charles;
When he had heard us,   he raised his hands on high
420   To praise his God,   but gave us no reply.
Now he has sent you   one of his noble lords,
A Count of France,   a man of power and wealth.
From him you'll learn   if there is hope for peace."
Marsile replies,   "We'll hear him; let him speak."

33

Count Ganelon   has taken careful thought,
Now he begins   in well-considered words,
Subtly contrived—   the Count knows how to talk.

---

425 ff. Ganelon is not only an accomplished liar but an enthusiastic one (see his description of the death of the Caliph, in *laisse* 54). Here only the tone would seem to misrepresent Charlemagne, except that Marsile will be allowed to keep only half of Spain, in fief to Charles; the other half is to be ruled by Roland. Thus the latter is made, once again, the focal point of the pagans' anger.

He tells Marsile: "May God grant you His grace,
That glorious Lord   to whom all men must pray!
Now by the will   of Charlemagne the King,   *430*
You must accept   the holy Christian law,
And half of Spain   he'll let you hold in fief.
Should you refuse   agreement to these terms,
You'll find yourself   a captive and in chains,
Taken by force   to answer Charles at Aix.
There you'll be judged,   and you will be condemned
To die a death   of infamy and shame."
At that Marsile   in fear and fury raised
A throwing spear—   its feathering was gold;
He would have struck,   but that his men took hold. AOI   *440*

34

In the King's face   they see the color change;
He stands there raging,   shaking his javelin.
Ganelon's hand   reaches to grasp his sword,
Out of the scabbard   draws it two finger lengths;
He tells the blade: "Shining you are, and fair!
Long have we served,   we two, at King Charles' court!
The Emperor of France   shall never say
I died alone   here in this foreign land
Before their best   have bought you at your price."
The pagans say,   "We must not let them fight!"   *450*

35

The Saracens   prevail upon Marsile
Until the King   will take his seat again.
Said the Caliph,   "You don't do any good
When you are ready   to strike the Frenchman down.
Just let him speak,   and listen to him well."
Ganelon says,   "My lord, I'll suffer that.

But I won't stop,   for all the gold God made,
For all the treasure   that's gathered in this land,
Before I give him,   if he will grant me time,
460   The message Charles   confided to my care,
The words he sends   his mortal enemy."
Ganelon wore   a cloak of sable furs
Covered in folds   of Alexandrian silk.
He throws it down—   it's caught by Blancandrin—
But has no thought   of letting go his sword:
His right hand grasps   the hilt made of bright gold.
The pagans say,   "Noble he is, and bold!" AOI

36

Count Ganelon   stands close beside the King,
And says to him,   "You have no cause for wrath
470   If Charlemagne   who rules the land of France
Says you must take   the holy Christian law:
One half of Spain   he'll let you hold in fief,
His nephew Roland   will rule the other part—
There you will have   a partner full of pride!
If you refuse   agreement to these terms,
In Saragossa   you soon will be beseiged,
You'll find yourself   a prisoner in chains,
And straight away   you'll be led off to Aix.
And then no palfrey,   no war-horse will you have,
480   Nor yet a mule   to ride with dignity,
But you'll be thrown   onto some pack-beast's back,
And lose your head   at that long journey's end.
Here is the message   I've brought at Charles' command."
He puts the letter   into Marsile's right hand.

37

Now King Marsile,   his face gone white with rage,
Breaks the seal open   and throws the wax away,

Looks at the letter   and sees what it contains.
"Thus writes King Charles   who rules the land of France:
He won't forget   his anger and his grief
About Basant   and his brother Basile   *490*
Whose heads I took   on a hill near Haltilie.
If I would make amends,   there's just one way:
I'll have to send him   my uncle, the Caliph;
If I refuse,   he'll have no love for me."
His son spoke up   and said to King Marsile,
"Wild empty words   we've had from Ganelon,
He's gone too far—   he well deserves to die.
Leave him to me,   and I'll do what is right."
Then Ganelon   prepared for the attack,
Brandished his sword,   the pine tree at his back.   *500*

38

Into an orchard   the pagan King retired,
And with him went   the wisest of his men.
Blancandrin came   whose heavy beard was grey,
And Jurfaret,   Marsile's own son and heir,
And the Caliph,   his uncle and good friend.
Says Blancandrin,   "Summon the Frenchman here—
I have his word   that he will serve our cause."
Marsile replies,   "Then bring him to me now."
Blancandrin takes   the Count by the right hand,
Walks through the orchard,   and leads him to Marsile.   *510*
They plot the treason   that cunning will conceal. AOI

39

Thus speaks the King: "My fair lord Ganelon,
I know I did   an ill-considered thing
When in my rage   I went to strike you down.
I pledge you now   by these fine sable furs—
The gold they're trimmed with   is worth five hundred pounds:

Tomorrow evening   I'll have made fair amends."
Says Ganelon,   "Your gift I won't refuse.
And if God please,   by this you shall not lose!" AOI

40

520   Then says Marsile,   "Know that I speak the truth,
Count Ganelon;   I want to be your friend.
Now will you tell me   something of Charlemagne.
Old as he is,   his time must have run out—
I know he's lived   more than two hundred years.
He has made journeys   to so many far lands,
So many blows   he's taken on his shield,
He has made beggars   of so many rich kings—
When will he ever   give up and take his rest?"
The Count replies,   "He's not as you suppose.
530   No one who sees him   and learns to know him well
Can fail to say   the Emperor is great.
My words won't give you   the measure of this man—
His noble virtues   are far beyond my praise—
And who could put   his courage into speech!
By God's grace, honor   illuminates my lord:
He'd rather die   than break faith with his court.

41

The pagan says,   "Truly, I am amazed
By Charlemagne   whose hair is grey with age—
I know he's lived   more than two hundred years.
540   He's dragged his body   through so many far lands,
Taken such blows   from lances and from spears,
So many kings   reduced to beggary,
It must be time   for him to look for peace."
"That will not happen   while Roland is alive;
There's no such vassal   under the high-domed sky;
And very brave   is Oliver his friend.

While the Twelve Peers   whom Charlemagne so loves
Serve as his vanguard   with twenty thousand knights,
The King is safe;   he fears no man alive." AOI

42

The pagan says,   "Now marvelous indeed   550
Is Charlemagne   whose hair has grown so white—
He is at least   two hundred years of age.
When he has conquered   so many distant lands,
Has taken blows   from so many sharp spears,
And such great kings   brought to defeat and death,
Is he not ready   to take his rest at home?"
The Count replies,   "Not while his nephew lives.
There's none so valiant   from here to the far East.
A great lord too   is Oliver his friend.
While the Twelve Peers,   for whom Charles feels such love, 560
Serve him and lead   those twenty thousand Franks,
Charles can be sure   no foe will break his ranks."

43

"Fair Ganelon,"   then says the pagan King,
"You'll see no soldiers   better at war than mine,
And I can summon   four hundred thousand knights.
Can I not fight   King Charles and all his Franks?"
"If you should try it,"   Count Ganelon replies,
"I tell you this,   you'd massacre your men.
Forget that folly,   and hear what I advise:
To Charlemagne   send such a royal gift   570
As to amaze   and gratify the French.
Send twenty men   as hostages for you,
And then the King   will go home to sweet France.
Behind his army   the rear-guard will remain,
And with them Roland,   the nephew of the King,
And Oliver,   so worthy and so brave.

And there they die—   if you'll do as I say.
King Charles will see   the downfall of his pride;
He'll have no wish   to carry on the fight." AOI

44

580   Answers Marsile,   "My fair lord Ganelon,
Tell me the way   Count Roland can be killed."
Ganelon says,   "Here is the plan I've made:
The King will cross   the mountain pass at Cize,
With a strong guard   remaining far behind.
He'll leave his nephew,   Count Roland, in the rear,
Oliver too,   in whom he has such faith,
With them a host   of twenty thousand Franks.
Then of your pagans,   a hundred thousand men
Must be sent out   to launch the first attack.
590   You'll see the Frenchmen   wounded and overcome—
Not that I say   your men won't suffer too.
If you attack   a second time that way,
You can be sure   that Roland won't escape.
Once you have done   this brave and knightly deed,
All your life long   from warfare you'll be freed."

45

"With that same blow   that struck Count Roland down,
You would cut off   the Emperor's right arm;
His mighty host   you'd scatter and destroy,
Nor would he find   so great a force again.
600   All of his Empire   would be restored to peace."
Marsile fell on his neck;   with joy he swore
That Ganelon   should loot his treasure-store. AOI

---

600. Following Jenkins I have translated *Tere Major* as "the Empire" throughout. Bédier calls it *la Terre des Aïeux*, "land of our fathers."

46

Then says Marsile,   "Why talk more . . .
There's no good counsel   unless . . .
Give me your oath   that Roland is to die."
"Just as you like!"   Count Ganelon replies.
He swore by relics   he carried in his sword, ⟧ Holy
And so forever   turned from his rightful lord. AOI
                        unholy

47

A throne was there,   made all of ivory.
A book was brought   by King Marsile's command: *610*
Laws of Mohammed   and Tervagant, his gods.
On this he swore,   the Spanish Saracen,
If he found Roland   was named to the rear-guard,
He would attack   with all his pagan knights,
And do his utmost   to see the Frenchman die.
"Amen to that!"   was Ganelon's reply.

48

There was a pagan,   his name was Valdabron,
He raised to knighthood   the Saracen Marsile.
Laughing for joy,   he said to Ganelon:
"Here is my sword,   a better you'll not find;   *620*
The hilt is worth   a thousand coins of gold!
I give you this   for friendship's sake, fair lord;
If you will help us,   we cannot fail to find
The valiant Roland   commanding the rear-guard."
The Count replies,   "You'll find him there, and win."
Then they exchange   kisses on cheek and chin.

---

603. Dots correspond to Segre's indication of illegible passages.

49

Afterward came   a man called Climborin.
Laughing for joy,   he said to Ganelon:
"Now take my helmet—   none better have I seen—
630   For with your help   in showing us the way,
We'll bring great Roland   to his defeat and shame."
Ganelon said,   "You won't have far to seek."
Then they exchanged   kisses on lips and cheek. AOI

50

Then came the Queen,   the lady Bramimonde.
"My lord," she said,   "I count myself your friend,
The King admires you,   and so do all his men.
Give to your wife   these necklaces from me,
Heavy with gold,   jacinths and amethysts—
A greater prize   than all the wealth of Rome,
640   And none so fine   has Charles who rules the Franks."
He put them in his boots,   and gave her thanks. AOI

51

Then the King summons   his treasurer Malduit:
"Have they prepared   the tribute for King Charles?"
"The seven hundred camels,   by your command,
Have all been loaded   with silver and with gold,
And twenty men,   our noblest, set to go." AOI

52

King Marsile places   his arm around the Count,
Saying to him,   "Valiant you are, and wise.

But as you keep   your God's most holy law,
I charge you never   to turn your heart from me!   *650*
Of all I own   I'll give you a good part:
Ten mules are loaded   with fine Arabian gold,
And every year   you'll have as much again.
Give Charles the keys   to this broad city's walls,
Tell him its treasures   will henceforth be his own,
And then have Roland   appointed to the guard.
If I can find him   crossing some narrow pass,
There I'll attack   and fight him to the death."
Ganelon says,   "Then let us speed the day."
He mounts his horse,   and quickly rides away. AOI   *660*

Scene 5

53

The Emperor Charles   has now retraced his steps
As far as Galne—   that was a captured town
Whose walls Count Roland   had leveled to the ground;
No one would live there   for the next hundred years.
He waits for news   of Ganelon's return,
And for the tribute   offered to him by Spain.
At dawn one morning,   just as the sky grows light,
Count Ganelon   comes back from his long ride. AOI

54

The Emperor Charles   rose early on that day.
Now, having prayed   at matins and a mass,   *670*
He goes outside   and stands on the green grass.
Roland is with him,   the noble Oliver,
Naimon the Duke,   and many others too.
Ganelon comes,   treacherous and forsworn.
All of his cunning   he puts into his speech,
Saying to Charles,   "I greet you in God's name!

Here are the keys   to King Marsile's fair town;
From Saragossa,   treasures beyond all price,
And twenty nobles,   hostages—guard them well!
680   But King Marsile   has asked me to explain
Why you won't see   his uncle, the Caliph:
Before my eyes   four hundred thousand men
All armed in mail,   some with their helmets closed,
Swords at their belts,   the hilts inlaid with gold,
Sailed with that lord   out to the open sea.
They fled because   they hated Christian law
Which they refused   to honor and to keep.
They sailed away,   but had not gone four leagues
When they were caught   in such a frightful storm
690   They all were drowned.   So perished the Caliph.
Were he alive,   he'd be here with me now.
As for Marsile,   my lord, you can be sure
That well before   a single month has passed,
He'll follow you   when you return to France.
There he'll accept   the Faith that you uphold,
Both of his hands   he'll place between your own,
And do you homage   for all his lands in Spain."
Then said the King,   "For this may God be thanked!
You have done well,   and great shall be your prize."
700   Among the hosts,   a thousand trumpets sound;
The French break camp,   they load each mule and horse,
And toward sweet France   they gladly set their course. AOI

55

King Charles the Great   has conquered all of Spain,
Captured its forts,   its cities laid to waste;
His war, he says,   has now come to its end.
The Emperor rides   once more toward his sweet France.
From Roland's spearhead   the flag of battle flies;

---

703. The poet returns to the beginning of his story, as also in line 2609.

When, from a hilltop,   it waves against the sky,
The French make camp   throughout the countryside.
Pagans are riding   through valleys deep and dark.   *710*
They wear their hauberks,   tunics of double chain,
Their helmets laced;   bright swords hang at their sides,
Shields at their necks,   a pennon on each lance.
Where trees grow thick   high on a hill they wait,
Four hundred thousand   watching for day's first light.
Alas! If only   the French could see that sight! AOI

56

The day is over,   the night grows calm and still.
The Emperor Charles   goes to his bed and sleeps.
In dream he rides   through the great pass at Cize;
Clasped in his hands   he holds an ashwood spear: *720*
Count Ganelon   wrenches it from his grasp,
And brandishes the spear   with such fierce strength,
He sends wood splinters   flying against the sky.
King Charles sleeps on,   not opening his eyes.

57

After that dream   another vision came:
He was in France,   in his chapel at Aix.
A vicious bear   was biting his right arm.
Out of the forest   he sees a leopard run,
And he himself   it cruelly attacks.
From his great hall   a swift hound gallops out   *730*
And comes to Charles,   running with leaps and bounds,
Seizes the bear,   biting its right ear off,
Then in its fury   attacks the leopard too.
The Frenchmen watch   the mighty battle rage,
But they don't know   which side will win the fight.
King Charles sleeps on,   and does not wake all night. AOI

58

Darkness of night   gives way to shining dawn.
Throughout the host,   clarion trumpets sound.
Proud, on his horse,   the Emperor appears.
740   "Barons, my lords,"   says Charlemagne the King,
"Narrow and dark   will be this mountain pass—
<u>Who shall remain   to guard us from the rear</u>?"
Ganelon says,   "Choose Roland, my stepson.
You have no baron   as valorous as he."
Fiercely the King   looks at the one who spoke,
And says to him: "Vile demon that you are!
You are insane,   possessed by deadly rage!
And in the vanguard—   who'll have the leader's place?"
Ganelon says,   "Count Ogier the Dane.
750   None would do better;   everyone knows his fame."

59

Count Roland heard   what Ganelon proposed,
And then he answered   with knightly courtesy:

746. *Vos estes vifs diables*. Brault believes that Charlemagne has a true intuition
that Ganelon made a pact with the devil—is a devil incarnate—and nevertheless
the Emperor, "determined to relive Abraham's agony" (p. 168), does not inter-
vene. There seem to me several difficulties about this view. If Charles thinks that
Ganelon is literally diabolical, he cannot at the same time feel obliged to further
his plans. On the other hand, if his words are merely an expression of his rage,
and if the interlocking events that have led to Ganelon's naming of Roland are
truly a manifestation of God's will, Charles still does not respond in the manner
of Abraham, or of Roland at Roncevaux, faced with a summons from God.
Rather he tries to ward off fate by consulting Naimon, accepts his useless advice,
and turns to the partial revelations of his dreams for confirmation of what he
knows in his heart. In any event, to "acknowledge his profound obligation to
play out his role as an Abraham figure" (Brault, p. 199) would seem to exclude
the absolute simplicity of Abraham's obedience when he is told to sacrifice
Isaac.

12 peers – chief officers

"Noble stepfather,   now I must hold you dear,
For you have named me   commander of this guard.
The King of France   won't lose by my neglect
War-horse or palfrey,   that I can promise you;
He shall not lose   a single riding-mule,
Saddle-horse, pack-horse—   none shall give up its life
Until our swords,   take payment for that prize."
Ganelon says,   "I know you tell no lies." AOI   760

60

When Roland heard   he'd stay with the rear-guard,
To his stepfather   he angrily replied:
"Ignoble serf,   despicable foul wretch,
Do you suppose   I'll let the glove fall here
The way you dropped the staff   at King Charles' feet?" AOI

61

"My rightful lord,"   says Roland to the King,
"Give me the bow   you're holding in your hand;
I promise you   that no man here will say
I let it fall,   like Ganelon that day
The envoy's staff   dropped out of his right hand."   770
The Emperor Charles   sits with his head bowed low,
Pulls his moustache,   and srokes his long white beard,
While in his eyes   unwilling tears appear.

Laisse 60. Segre agrees with other editors, including Jenkins, that this *laisse*, which occurs only in the Oxford Manuscript, may not be authentic. Scribal attempts to be consistent could account for the repetition of its details in the two *laisses* that follow (the dropping of a staff, Roland's anger).

773. Although Charlemagne tries to restrain his tears, they obviously do him credit: sensitivity was no sign of weakness in a warrior. Roland, in *laisse* 140, weeps for the dead Franks "like a noble knight."

62

At that Duke Naimon   stood up to speak his mind—
The court could boast   no better man than he—
Saying to Charles,   "You have heard what's been said;
It's not surprising   that Roland is enraged:
He has been named   to go with the rear-guard.
You have no baron   who will dispute that now.
780 Give him the bow   that you yourself have bent;
Then choose good men   to fight at his command."
King Charles has put the bow   in Roland's hand.

63

The Emperor Charles   calls Roland to come forth.
"My noble nephew,   this is what I intend:
Half of my army   shall stay behind with you.
Accept their service,   and then you will be safe."
Count Roland answers,   "Never will I agree.
May God destroy me,   if I so shame my race!
Just twenty thousand   shall serve me, valiant Franks.
790 You'll cross the mountains,   safely in France arrive—
And fear no man   as long as I'm alive!"

64

Roland has mounted   the horse he rides to war. AOI
There comes to join him   his friend Count Oliver,
And Gerin comes,   the brave Count Gerier,
And Oton comes,   with him Count Berenger,
And Astor comes,   and fiery Anseïs,
And old Gérard,   the Count of Roussillon,

---

774. Duke Naimon's advice is always followed, usually to disaster.

The powerful and wealthy   Duke Gaïfier.
Says the Archbishop,   "My head on it, I'll go!"
"And I am with you,"   answers Count Gautier,   *800*
"I'm Roland's vassal—   my help is his by right."
Then they select   the twenty thousand knights. AOI

65

Count Roland says   to Gautier de l'Hum:
"A thousand Franks,   men of our land, you'll take
To occupy   the hills and the ravines,
So that King Charles   may safely go his way." AOI
Gautier answers,   "For you I'll do my best."
Leading away   a thousand Franks of France,
Gautier will guard   the mountains and ravines;
Whatever happens,   he won't come down again   *810*
Without a battle—   Almaris of Belferne
Gave them a fight,   and seven hundred blades
Flashed from their scabbards   on that most evil day.

Act II

66

High are the hills,   the valleys shadowy;
The cliffs rise grey,   the narrow ways hold fear.
The French ride on   in misery and pain,
Their passing heard   some fifteen leagues around;
And when once more   they're back again in France,
In Gascony,   where Charlemagne is lord,
Then they remember   the lands they hold, their sons,   *820*
Their maiden daughters,   their fair and noble wives—
There is not one   who is not moved to weep.
But of them all   none sorrows as does Charles,
For he has left   his nephew there in Spain;
And now his tears   the King cannot restrain. AOI

67

All the Twelve Peers   have stayed behind in Spain;
They guard the pass   with twenty thousand Franks,
Courageous men   who do not fear to die.
And now King Charles   is riding home again;
830   He drapes his cloak   to hide his grieving face.
Duke Naimon rides   next to the Emperor;
He says to Charles,   "What weighs your spirits down?"
The King replies,   "Who asks me that does wrong.
I can't keep silent   the sorrow that I feel,
For Ganelon   will be the doom of France.
Last night an angel   sent me a warning dream:
I held a spear—   he broke it from my grasp,
That Count who named   my nephew to the guard.
And I left Roland   among that pagan race—
840   God! If I lose him,   no one can take his place." AOI

68

Charlemagne weeps;   he can't hold back his tears.
They grieve for him,   his hundred thousand Franks,
And for Count Roland   are suddenly afraid.
A traitor's lies   left him to die in Spain—
Rich gifts the pagan   bestowed on Ganelon:
Silver and gold,   brocades and silken cloaks,
Camels and lions,   fine horses, riding mules.
Now King Marsile   summons the lords of Spain,
His counts and viscounts,   his chieftains and his dukes,
850   His high emirs,   and all their warrior sons:
Four hundred thousand   assemble in three days.
In Saragossa   the drums begin to sound;
They place Mohammed   high on the citadel—

---

848. This admirable transition should be noted: from the unproven but accurate
presentiments of the Franks to the actual preparations of Marsile.

No pagan fails   to worship him and pray.
And then they ride   with all their might and main
Searching the land,   through valleys, over hills,
Until they see   the battle-flags of France.
The Twelve Companions   are waiting with the guard;
When they are challenged,   the fighting will be hard.

69

King Marsile's nephew   rides up before the host.   *860*
Laughing, he prods his mule   with a sharp goad,
And to his uncle   addresses this fair speech:
"For years, Lord King,   I've served you faithfully;
My only wages   were hardships, suffering,
And battles fought   and won on many fields.
I ask this boon: have Roland left to me!
I'll take his life   on my sharp-pointed spear,
And if Mohammed   protects me in the fight,
The whole of Spain   once more shall be our own,
From the high passes   as far as Durestant!   *870*
Charles will be weary,   the Frenchmen will retreat;
In all your lifetime,   war will not touch your land."
King Marsile places   the gauntlet in his hand. AOI

70

King Marsile's nephew,   the gauntlet in his fist,
Speaks to his uncle   in proud and fiery words:
"You've given me,   fair Sire, a noble gift.
Choose for me now   the twelve among your lords
Who'll meet in battle   with the Twelve Peers of France."

866. Marsile's nephew, whose name we learn later is Aelroth, asks for first blow
against Roland.
877. Including himself, as the Twelve French Peers include Roland.

First of them all,   Duke Falsaron replies—
880   This Saracen   was brother to Marsile—
He says, "Fair nephew,   both you and I will go,
And they'll find out   what fighting really means.
The rear-guard waits,   protecting Charlemagne;
When we attack,   those Franks will all be slain!" AOI

71

King Corsablis   comes forward in his turn.
He is a Berber,   and skilled in the black arts.
He speaks up now,   a vassal true and brave—
For all God's gold,   he'd never run away.
Spurring, there comes   Malprimis of Brigant,
890   Faster on foot   than any horse can run.
Before Marsile   he stands and shouts aloud:
"At Roncevaux   my war-cry shall resound—
If I find Roland,   I'll leave him on the ground!" AOI

72

Comes an Emir,   the lord of Balaguer,
A handsome man,   his face serene and bold.
Whoever sees him   riding his horse to war,
Bearing his arms   with courage and great pride,
Knows that this hero   well deserves his fame;
If he were Christian,   he'd be a noble knight.
900   Before Marsile   he stops and cries aloud,
"I'll go my way   to Roncevaux and fight!
If I find Roland,   there he shall lose his life,
Oliver too,   and all of the Twelve Peers.
The French will die   in sorrow and great shame.
Now Charlemagne grows old,   weak in his mind;
He'll have no wish   to carry on the war—
In all of Spain   we'll see no more of Franks."
For that fair speech,   Marsile gave many thanks. AOI

Twelve Peers   now stand condemned to die;
ench are lost—   soon France will feel their lack—
s will be needing   good vassals at his back." AOI

6

n rides forth   the pagan Estorgant—
rn companion   Estramariz comes too—
tors both,   famed for they lying tongues.
ys the King,   "Come forward, my good lords!
e mountains   you'll ride to Roncevaux,
your place   as leaders of my men."
y reply,   "My lord, at your command!
attack   Roland and Oliver;
can save   the Twelve Peers from swift death.
our swords,   keen are their blades and strong;
will stain them   bright crimson with hot blood!
ch will die,   and Charlemagne know grief,
Empire   we'll give you for your own.
ith us, Sire,   and witness their defeat—
ve King Charles,   a captive, at your feet."

comes running   Margariz of Seville—
e land   as far as Cazmarines—
handsome   no lady can resist:
his presence,   but feels inclined toward love,
she sees him   refuses him a smile.
best   of all the pagan knights.

ost charming of the pagans—perhaps of all the knights—Margariz
not die on the battlefield, but vanishes, at least from the Oxford
after attacking Oliver (1318). Evidence from other versions suggest-
that Margariz was spared to be the messenger who would tell
ate of his first army.

73

Then an Emir   who came from Mor
There was no man   more evil in all
Rode to Marsile   and made his boas
"To Roncevaux   I'll lead my compa
All twenty thousand   with lances a
If I find Roland,   his death is a sure
And every day   that loss will griev

74

And then rides forth   Turgis of Tu
He is a Count,   the ruler of that t
His heart desires   to work the Ch
And with the others   he stands b
Telling the King: "We'll triumph
Against Mohammed,   Saint Peter
Give him your prayers,   and we
At Roncevaux,   Roland shall me
And then no man   can save him
Look at my sword—   how keen
When this blade strikes   against
You'll soon be hearing   which
The Franks will die   who meet
Leaving old Charles,   whom sh
To live his days   a King withou

75

And then rides forth   Escrimiz
That is the fief   held by this S
His voice rings out   above the
"At Roncevaux   I'll bring the
If I find Roland,   he won't le
Nor Oliver,   who leads so ma

All the
The Fr
Charle

7

940   And th
His sw
Fell tra
Then s
Over th
Taking
And the
We will
Nothing
Here ar
950   Soon we
The Fre
All of his
Come w
We'll ha

77

And the
He has t
A man s
None, in
Or when
960   He is the

*955. The m
alone does
Manuscript,
ed to Bédie
Marsile the f

His voice rings out   above the swelling crowd
To tell the King,   "Now have no fear, my lord!
At Roncevaux   Count Roland will be slain
By my own hand,   as Oliver shall die;
The Twelve Peers all   shall have their martyrdom.
Look at my sword—   its hilt is made of gold—
A noble gift   from the Emir of Primes;
I swear to you   I'll sheathe it in red blood.
The Franks will die,   and France be brought to shame.
Old Charlemagne   whose flowing beard is white   *970*
Shall live his days   in sorrow and in wrath.
Within a year   we'll conquer all of France—
We'll go to bed   in Saint Denis' own town."
The pagan King,   in gratitude, bows down. AOI

78

And then comes forward   Chernuble of Muneigre;
His hair's so long   it sweeps the very ground.
Sometimes, for fun,   he'll carry on his back
Burdens enough   to overload four mules.
In that far country   from which he comes, they say
The sun won't shine,   no wheat will ever grow,   *980*
Rain never falls,   nor is there any dew;
The rocks and stones   in all the land are black:
Some, for that reason,   call it the devil's home.
Chernuble says,   "My sword is at my side;
At Roncevaux,   I'll stain its keen blade red.
If I should find   great Roland on my way,
I'll challenge him—   or trust me not again—
And my sharp blade   will conquer Durendal.
The Franks will die,   and France see them no more."
And at these words   the Twelve Peers take command.   *990*
They lead away   a hundred thousand men,
All of them eager   to form the battle lines.
They put on armor,   inside a grove of pines.

79

The pagans wear   Saracen coats of mail,
Most of them furnished   with triple-layered chain.
From Saragossa   come the good helms they lace;
They gird on swords   whose steel comes from Vienne.
Their shields are strong;   Valencia made their spears;
Their battle flags   are crimson, blue and white.
1000   All mules and palfreys   must now be left behind.
Each mounts his war-horse;   in close-knit ranks they ride.
Fair is the day,   the sun shines bright and clear,
Weapons and armor   glitter with fiery light,
A thousand trumpets   command more splendor still.
That great shrill clamor   reaches the Frenchmen's camp.
Oliver says,   "Companion, it would seem
That we will have   some Saracens to fight."
Roland replies,   "God grant that you be right!
Here we will stand,   defending our great King.
1010   This is the service   a vassal owes his lord:
To suffer hardships,   endure great heat and cold,
And in a battle   to lose both hair and hide.
Now every Frank   prepare to strike great blows—
Let's hear no songs   that mock us to our shame!
Pagans are wrong,   the Christian cause is right.
A bad example   I'll be in no man's sight." AOI

80

Count Oliver   has climbed up on a hill.
From there he searches   the valley to his right,
And sees that host   of pagan Saracens.
1020   Then he calls out   to Roland, his sworn friend:
"Coming from Spain   I see the fiery glow
Of shining hauberks,   the blazing steel of helms.
For our brave Franks   this means great toil and pain.
And that foul traitor,   false-hearted Ganelon,
Knew this—that's why   he named us to the guard."

Count Roland answers,   "Stop, Oliver, be still!
Of my stepfather   I'll let no man speak ill."

81

Count Oliver   has climbed up on a hill;
From there he sees   the Spanish lands below,
And Saracens   assembled in great force.   *1030*
Their helmets gleam   with gold and precious stones,
Their shields are shining,   their hauberks burnished gold,
Their long sharp spears   with battle flags unfurled.
He tries to see   how many men there are:
Even battalions   are more than he can count.
And in his heart,   Oliver is dismayed;
Quick as he can,   he comes down from the height,
And tells the Franks   what they will have to fight.

82

Oliver says,   "Here come the Saracens—
A greater number   no man has ever seen!   *1040*
The first host carries   a hundred thousand shields.
Their helms are laced,   their hauberks shining bright,
From straight wood handles   rise ranks of burnished spears.
You'll have a battle   like none on earth before!
Frenchmen, my lords,   now God give you the strength
To stand your ground,   and keep us from defeat."
They say, "God's curse   on those who quit the field!
We're yours till death—   not one of us will yield." AOI

83

Oliver says,   "The pagan might is great—
It seems to me,   our Franks are very few!   *1050*
Roland, my friend,   it's time to sound your horn;

King Charles will hear,   and bring his army back."
Roland replies,   "You must think I've gone mad!
In all sweet France   I'd forfeit my good name!
No! I will strike   great blows with Durendal,
Crimson the blade   up to the hilt of gold.
To those foul pagans   I promise bitter woe—
They all are doomed   to die at Roncevaux!" AOI

84

𝕀

"Roland, my friend,   let the Oliphant sound!
1060   King Charles will hear it,   his host will all turn back,
His valiant barons   will help us in this fight."
Roland replies,   "Almighty God forbid
That I bring shame   upon my family,
And cause sweet France   to fall into disgrace!
I'll strike that horde   with my good Durendal;
My sword is ready,   girded here at my side,
And soon you'll see   its keen blade dripping blood.
The Saracens   will curse the evil day
They challenged us,   for we will make them pay." AOI

85

𝕀𝕀

1070   "Roland, my friend,   I pray you, sound your horn!
King Charlemagne,   crossing the mountain pass,
Won't fail, I swear it,   to bring back all his Franks."
"May God forbid!"   Count Roland answers then.
"No man on earth   shall have the right to say
That I for pagans   sounded the Oliphant!
I will not bring   my family to shame.
I'll fight this battle;   my Durendal shall strike
A thousand blows   and seven hundred more;

1059. Roland's famous horn, made of ivory.

You'll see bright blood   flow from the blade's keen steel.
We have good men;   their prowess will prevail,   *1080*
And not one Spaniard   shall live to tell the tale."

86

Oliver says,   "Never would you be blamed;
I've seen the pagans,   the Saracens of Spain.
They fill the valleys,   cover the mountain peaks;
On every hill,   and every wide-spread plain,
Vast hosts assemble   from that alien race;
Our company   numbers but very few."
Roland replies,   "The better, then, we'll fight!
The saints and angels,   almighty God forbid
That I betray   the glory of sweet France!   *1090*
Better to die   than learn to live with shame—
Charles loves us more   as our keen swords win fame."

87

Roland's a hero,   and Oliver is wise;   ] *Roland's flaw = lack of wisdom*
Both are so brave   men marvel at their deeds.
When they mount chargers,   take up their swords and shields,
Not death itself   could drive them from the field.

prowess
1093. Rollant est proz e Oliver est sage. Bédier's translation of *proz* as *preux*,
wisdom
and *sage* as *sage* contributed much to the misunderstanding of these words,
both in themselves and in their supposed opposition to each other. In modern
French *preux* there is only the idea of valor, while *sage* means not only wise but
prudent, moderate. Both words in Old French are used differently: *proz* includes
the capacity for giving good counsel first mentioned in connection with
Blancandrin (26); *sage* does not involve the idea of prudence or moderation.
Brault points out that Bédier translates the two words as interchangeable: *proz*
equals *preux* (1209), and *sage* (2423) (*The Song of Roland*, p. 413, note 28).
This seems to acknowledge the idea of wisdom in *prozdom*. Archbishop Turpin,
(3691), is both *proz* and *sage*.

They are good men;   their words are fierce and proud.
With wrathful speed   the pagans ride to war.
Oliver says,   "Roland, you see them now.
1100   They're very close,   the King too far away.
You were too proud   to sound the Oliphant:
If Charles were with us,   we would not come to grief.
Just look up there!   Close to the Aspre Pass,
The rear-guard stands,   grieving for what must come.
To fight this battle   means not to fight again."
Roland replies,   "Don't speak so foolishly!
Cursed be the heart   that cowers in the breast!
We'll hold our ground;   if they will meet us here,
Our foes will find us   ready with sword and spear." AOI

88

1110   When Roland sees   the fight will soon begin,
Lions and leopards   are not so fierce as he.
Calling the Franks,   he says to Oliver:
"Noble companion,   my friend, don't talk that way!
The Emperor Charles,   who left us in command
Of twenty thousand   he chose to guard the pass,
Made very sure   no coward's in their ranks.
In his lord's service   a man must suffer pain,

The general intention of the *laisse* is to indicate the equality of the two warriors, their awe-inspiring courage. This may have been apparent to medieval readers even in the first line, but it is difficult to express in English. There is really no choice about "wise." *Proz* has been rendered in a variety of ways from "fierce" (Sayers) to "good" (Goldin). Brault says its basic meaning is "worthy." I feel that "good" and "worthy" do not properly balance "wise," a weightier word. Consequently I have chosen to express the particular aspect of Roland's *prozdom*, which, although he specifically shares it, in terms of courage, with Oliver, nevertheless can distinguish Roland most particularly. The wisdom of heroes is different from, but at least equal to, the voice of reason.

Bitterest cold   and burning heat endure;
He must be willing   to lose his flesh and blood.
Strike with your lance,   and I'll wield Durendal—   *1120*
The King himself   presented it to me—
And if I die,   whoever takes my sword
Can say its master   has nobly served his lord."

89

Archbishop Turpin   comes forward then to speak.
He spurs his horse   and gallops up a hill,
Summons the Franks,   and preaches in these words:
"My noble lords,   Charlemagne left us here,
And may our deaths   do honor to the King!
Now you must help   defend our holy Faith!
War is upon us—   I need not tell you that—   *1130*
Before your eyes   you see the Saracens
Confess your sins,   ask God to pardon you;
I'll grant you absolution   to save your souls.
If you should die,   that will be martyrdom,
And you'll have places   in highest Paradise."
The French dismount;   they kneel upon the ground.
Then the Archbishop,   blessing them in God's name,
Told them, for penance,   to strike when battle came.

[handwritten margin notes:] Reconciliation
—forgiveness
—payment
1) Contrition
2) Confession
3) Satisfaction

90

[handwritten note:] fighting —an act pleasing to God.
→ Crusades

The kneeling Franks   have risen to their feet.
They are absolved,   and free from any sin;   *1140*
Archbishop Turpin   has signed them with the cross.
Now they have mounted   swift horses bred for war;
They bear the weapons   befitting them as knights.
Thus they await   the Saracen attack.
Count Roland calls   Oliver to his side:

"My lord companion,   the words you spoke were true;
This is the work   of faithless Ganelon—
He sold us all   for treasure, gold and coins.
Now may he suffer   the Emperor's revenge!
1150 As for the bargain   that King Marsile has made,
Without good swords,   he'll forfeit what he paid." AOI

91

At Roncevaux   Count Roland passes by,
Riding his charger,   swift-running Veillantif.
He's armed for battle,   splendid in shining mail.
As he parades,   he brandishes his lance,
Turning the point   straight up against the sky,
And from the spearhead   a banner flies, pure white,
With long gold fringes   that beat against his hands.
Radiant, fair to see,   he laughs for joy.
1160 Now close behind him   comes Oliver, his friend,
With all the Frenchmen   cheering their mighty lord.
Fiercely his eyes   confront the Saracens;
Respectfully, fondly   he gazes at the Franks,
Speaking these gallant words   to cheer their hearts:
"Barons, my lords,   softly now, keep the pace!
Here come the pagans   looking for martyrdom.
We'll have such plunder   before the day is out,

1152. "At Roncevaux," *as porz d'Espaigne*—the pass, the "gates of Spain."
1161. They acclaim him as their *guarant*, protector.
1167. "Plunder": *eschec*. The word derives from the Germanic *schâch*, meaning "booty." According to Brault, it can also mean "battle." I think that Roland, convinced (correctly as it turns out) that his few men can destroy the Saracen army, uses *eschec* in its usual, material, sense. Cook and Brault both prefer to see here a promise of spiritual reward, but military victory, plunder included, would be the first hope of soldiers, no matter how holy their war. The participants do not yet know that the French will be rewarded only by martyrdom. In any case, I do not believe Roland capable of deliberately misleading speech.

As no French king   has ever won before!"
And at this moment   the armies join in war. AOI

92

Oliver says,   "I have no heart for words.   *1170*
You were too proud   to sound the Oliphant:
No help at all   you'll have from Charlemagne.
It's not his fault—   he doesn't know our plight,
Nor will the men   here with us be to blame.
But now, ride on,   to fight as you know how.
Barons, my lords,   in battle hold your ground!
And in God's name,   I charge you, be resolved
To strike great blows   for those you have to take.
Let's not forget   the war-cry of King Charles!"
He says these words,   and all the Franks cry out;   *1180*
No one who heard   that mighty shout, "Montjoie!"
Would soon forget   the valor of these men.
And then, how fiercely,   God! they begin to ride,
Spurring their horses   to give their utmost speed,
They race to strike—   what else is there to do?
The Saracens stand firm;   they won't retreat.
Pagans and Christians,   behold! in battle meet.

93

King Marsile's nephew,   Aelroth is his name,
First of the pagans,   rides out before the host,
Taunting our Franks   with loud malicious words: *1190*
"Today, foul Frenchmen,   you'll break a lance with us;

1174. This line could equally well mean: "Nor will the men with Charles be to blame."
1181. "Montjoie"—the poet of the *Roland* explains its origin (*Laisses* 183 and 225). Jenkins suggests also the pilgrims' cry of joy on seeing the end of their quest for Monte Gaudia or a similar hill near Jerusalem or Santiago.

You stand here now   abandoned and betrayed!
The King was mad   to leave you at the pass:
This day sweet France   will see its pride cast down.
The Emperor Charles   will lose his good right arm!"
Count Roland hears him,   God! with what pain and rage!
He spurs his horse   to run with all its might,
Levels his lance,   strikes Aelroth such a blow
His shield is shattered,   the hauberk split in two,
1200   The pagan's bones   crack open in his chest,
His broken spine   sticks out behind his back
So that the spear   drives out his very soul.
Under the thrust   the body starts to fall,
And Roland hurls him   a spear's length from his horse;
He falls down dead,   his neck broken in two.
But still Count Roland   gives him these parting words:
"Foul infidel,   King Charles is not a fool,
Nor was he ever   unfaithful to his trust.
Wisely he chose   that we should guard the pass;
1210   Sweet France will lose   no glory here today.
Strike on, you Franks!   First blood will win the fight!
Their cause is evil,   and we are in the right." AOI

94

A Duke is there   whose name is Falsaron,
Aelroth's uncle,   brother to King Marsile:
Dathan was his,   and he held Abirun—
No man more ruthless   was ever seen on earth.
He was a giant: his forehead, monstrous wide,
A good six inches   measured from eye to eye.
Because he grieves   to see his nephew dead,
1220   He rushes forward   to challenge any foe,
All the while shouting   the pagan battle-cry.
In his great fury   he challenges the Franks:
"Today sweet France   will see its honor fall!"
Oliver hears this,   and mightily enraged,

Pricking his horse   with spurs of shining gold,
Charges to strike him,   as a true knight would do.
The shield cracks open,   the hauberk splits apart,
Up to the pennon   the spear-head drives on through;
Thrust from his saddle,   Falsaron hits the ground.
The Count looks down   to see the scoundrel die,   *1230*
And speaks to him   in proud and fiery words:
"You know now, felon,   how much I heed your threats!
Strike on, you Franks!   They've come here to be slain."
"Montjoie!" he shouts,   the cry of Charlemagne. AOI

95

A King is there,   his name is Corsablis,
From Barbary,   that land across the sea.
He shouts this counsel   to cheer the Saracens:
"Here is a battle   easy enough to win
When so few Franks   are left to guard the pass
What can we do   but hold them in contempt?   *1240*
Charles has no power   to save a single one:
This is the day   when they are doomed to die."
Archbishop Turpin   has heard him make this boast;
In all the world   he hates no man so much.
Pricking his horse   with spurs of purest gold,
He strikes the Berber   such a tremendous blow
His shield splits open,   the chain-mail flies apart,
Turpin's great spear   comes out beyond his back,
And falling backward   under that awful thrust,
Corsablis lands   a spear's length from his horse.   *1250*
Turpin looks down,   and sees that vile wretch die,
Nor will he leave   before he tells him this:
"Foul infidel,   you made your boast with lies.

1226. The expression *en guise de baron* occurs very often in the text, and would seem to be simply a way of saying "valiantly." See also lines 1889 and 1902.

Who serves King Charles   is ever safe from harm,
And of our Franks   not one would wish to flee.
All your companions   will soon be put to rest.
You will discover   there's no way out but death.
Strike, men of France!   Forget not who you are!
Thanks be to God,   first blood is on our side."
1260   And then "Montjoie!"   to claim the field, he cried.

96

Count Gerin strikes   Malprimis of Brigant
Whose great stout shield   proves not worth half a cent:
The blow, dead center,   shatters the crystal boss,
And half the shield   goes crashing to the ground;
Right through the hauberk   the heavy spearhead thrusts,
Pierces the flesh,   and lodges deep inside.
The wretched pagan   falls in a crumpled heap;
A devil carries   his soul away to keep. AOI

97

Then the Emir   is struck by Gerier
1270   Who breaks his shield   and shatters his chain-mail,
Pierces his body   with a great thrust of steel
Until the spearhead   comes out the other side.
Balaguer falls   a spear's length from his horse.
Oliver says,   "Valor will beat their force!"

98

Moriane's Emir   receives Duke Samson's charge;
Flowers and gold   will not defend his shield,

1269. The Emir of Balaguer.

Nor will his chain-mail   do him a bit of good.
His heart cut open,   his liver and his lungs,
He falls down dead,   if any care or no.
Says the Archbishop,   "That was a baron's blow!"   *1280*

99

Then Anseïs   charges on his swift horse;
When his spear strikes   Turgis of Turtelusc,
The shield cracks open   below the golden boss,
The double hauberk   splits open, snaps apart,
The spearhead thrusts   into the pagan's flesh
Until the point   comes out beyond his back.
Turgis falls dead,   face down upon the field.
Count Roland says,   "That was a hero's deed."

100

The Gascon knight,   Engelier of Bordeaux,
Spurs on his horse,   and lets him have his head,   *1290*
Charging to strike   Escremiz of Valterne.
He cracks the shield   hung round the pagan's neck,
Pierces the hauberk   just where the flap is laced,
Thrusts through his chest   between the collarbones,
And fells him dead   a spear's length from his horse.
Engelier says,   "For death you set your course." AOI

101

Then Oton strikes   the pagan Estorgant,
Hitting his shield   hard on the upper edge,
He cuts its quarters   the crimson and the white;
The hauberk cracks   where the two halves are joined,   *1300*

1280. Baron is used nonspecifically to refer to a nobleman or a hero.

The shining spear-point   thrusts deep into his flesh.
Thrown from his charger,   he lies dead on the ground,
And Oton says,   "See who will save you now!"

102

Then Berenger   charges Estramariz,
Shatters his spear,   splits the chain-mail apart;
He drives his spear-point   deep through the pagan's flesh,
Fells him among   a thousand Saracens.
The Franks have killed   ten of the pagan Peers;
These two alone   have not come to defeat:
1310   One is Chernuble,   the other Margariz.

103

That valiant knight,   Margariz of Seville,
Handsome and strong,   agile and very quick,
Spurs on his horse   and charges Oliver,
Piercing his shield   under its boss of gold
So that the spear-point   grazes his very ribs.
The hand of God   has turned aside that thrust,
The shaft is broken;   Oliver does not fall.
Margariz gallops on,   right through the Franks,
And blows his trumpet   to cheer the pagan ranks.

104

1320   Now wondrous battle   rages throughout the field.
Roland fights on,   not caring to keep safe,
Strikes with his spear   until the shaft is gone—
And fifteen blows   it gave before it broke.
Then from its scabbard   he draws great Durendal,

Spurs on and charges   Chernuble of Muneigre,
Slashing his helmet   where the bright rubies gleam,
Slices his hood   and downward through his hair,
Between the eyes   he cuts his face in two,
Through the bright hauberk,   of tightly-woven mail,
And all his body   down to the groin is split.   *1330*
Then through the saddle   adorned with threads of gold,
The sword drives deep   into the pagan's horse,
Cleaving the spine   where there's a joint or no—
Both man and beast   fall dead in thick green grass.
Then Roland says,   "Foul serf, you've found your doom.
See how Mohammed   protects you in the fray!
No man so vile   will win this fight today."

105

Count Roland gallops   everywhere in the field
With Durendal,   well-made to slash and cleave.
Great is the havoc   among the Saracens—   *1340*
One on the other   he heaps their bodies high!
The bright blood flows   streaming along the ground;
Roland's hauberk   and both his arms are red,
The neck and shoulders   of his good charger too.
Count Oliver   fights on and never stops;
The other Peers,   like him, deserve all praise.
The valiant Franks   strike and cut down their foes;
The pagans die,   or stricken, fall and faint.
Says the Archbishop,   "God's blessing be their thanks!"
He shouts, "Montjoie!"   the war-cry of the Franks. AOI   *1350*

1326. The red jewels here designated as rubies are called *carbuncle* throughout
the text. The word is derived from Latin *carbo* (coal), and, by extension, glow-
ing coal or ember, as in *escarbuner,* to shine like burning coal, (Godefroy). It
refers to any of several red gems.

106

Oliver rides   through the thick of the fray;
His spear is shattered,   only a stump remains.
He gallops on,   and charges Malsarun,
Breaking his shield   bright with flowers and gold.
The pagan's eyes   are thrust out of his head,
Parts of his brain   stream down him to his feet;
He goes to join   the seven hundred slain.
Oliver kills   Turgis and Esturgus;
The spear-shaft breaks   and splinters in his hands.
1360   Then Roland says,   "What are you doing, friend?
For such a battle   why did you choose a stick?
I'll take my chances   with iron and stout steel!
Where is your sword,   the one you call Halteclere,
With crystal hilt   and guard of shining gold?"
"I had no time," he says,   "to draw my sword,
With all those pagans   to send to their reward!" AOI

107

Lord Oliver   has drawn his good Halteclere,
The sword that Roland   was asking him to use,
And shows its powers   in a most knightly way:
1370   He rides to strike   Justin of Val Ferrée—
With just one blow   he splits that pagan's head,
Cleaves through the body,   the brightly polished mail,
The splendid saddle   sparkling with gold and jewels,
And breaks the spine   of Justin's war-horse too;
Both bodies fall   into the meadow grass.
And Roland says,   "That's my true brother now!
For such great blows   Charlemagne holds us dear."
Then from all sides,   "Montjoie!" the Frenchmen cheer. AOI

108

Count Gerin rides   a horse he calls Sorel,
With Gerier,   his friend, on Passecerf;   *1380*
They loosen reins   and spur their horses on,
Racing to charge   the pagan Timozel.
One strikes the hauberk,   the other hits the shield,
Both of their spears,   deep in his body, break;
He's thrown off backward,   dead, in a fallow field.
Which was the faster   of these two chevaliers?
I haven't heard,   and certainly can't tell.
Eperveris,   whose father was Burel,
Then met his slayer,   the Gascon Engelier.
Archbishop Turpin   has slaughtered Siglorel;   *1390*
The great enchanter   went once before to Hell—
That time by magic,   with Jupiter as guide.
Then Turpin says,   "I think he was no friend!"
And Roland answers,   "To death that villain goes.
Oliver, brother,   I love to see such blows!"

109

Meanwhile the battle   grows hotter all the time,
Both Franks and pagans   exchange prodigious blows;
Some charge and strike,   others defend their lives.
Spears without number   are shattered, stained with blood,
Pennons are ripped,   and battle-flags destroyed!   *1400*
So many Franks   who lay down their young lives
Will not return   to mothers or to wives

1392. Jenkins points out that Jupiter, like Apollo in line 8, is a demon. But the
latter is worshiped as a god, if only by the Saracens. Classical nomenclature in
the *Roland* is no more reliable than the poet's geography.

Or to those waiting   beyond the Gates of Spain.
King Charlemagne   will weep for bitter woe;
What good are tears?   His help will come too late.
Ill was he served   by Ganelon that day
In Saragossa;   he sold the King's own men.
For that betrayal,   he lost his life and limbs;
The trial at Aix   condemned him to be hanged
1410   His thirty kinsmen   also were forced to pay.
They never thought   their lives would end that way. AOI

110

Now fierce and grim   the battle rages on.
Oliver, Roland—   how valiantly they fight!
Turpin delivers   more than a thousand blows;
Among the Peers   none dreams of holding back,
And all together,   the Franks, as one man, strike.
By hundreds, thousands,   the pagans fall and die;
There's no way out   except for those who flee:
Each one who stays   is living his last day.
1420   But others die—   the best among the Franks—
They'll never see   their families again,
Or Charlemagne   who waits beyond the pass.
A fearful storm   that very day strikes France;
Through rushing winds   long peals of thunder roar,
And heavy rains,   enormous hailstones fall,
Great bolts of lightning   are striking everywhere.
Now the whole earth   is trembling dreadfully
From Saint Michel   all the way down to Sens,
From Besançon   to Wissant on the sea;
1430   There is no stronghold   without a shattered wall.
At noontime shadows   darken the light of day;
The only brightness   comes when the black sky cracks,
And no man sees it   who isn't terrified.
Many declare,   "The world is at an end—
The Day of Wrath   has come upon us now!"

But they know nothing,   and they believe a lie.
The heavens grieve   that Roland is to die.

111

The Franks of France   have struck with mighty force;
Enormous numbers   of Saracens are slain:
A hundred thousand,   and just one man remains.   *1440*
Says the Archbishop,   "Our Franks are brave and true;
No king on earth   can boast of better men.
Gesta Francorum   says of our Emperor
That all his vassals   were valorous and brave."
They walk the field,   searching among the dead;
For grief and pity   they cannot help but weep,
Thinking of those   whose loved ones won't come back.
Then King Marsile   launches a new attack. AOI

112

Now King Marsile   through a deep valley rides
With the great host   he summoned to his aid: *1450*
Twenty battalions   march with the Saracen.
Their helmets gleam   with gold and precious stones,
Bright are their shields,   their hauberks saffron-gold.
With seven hundred trumpets   sounding the charge,
Their coming echoes   for many miles around.
Then Roland says,   "Oliver, brother, friend,
Foul Ganelon   has sent us to our deaths;
But his betrayal   can never be concealed,
And we can leave   our vengence to King Charles.
We'll have a battle   to try our utmost strength,   *1460*

1440. The one remaining pagan is presumably Margariz.
1443. Gesta Francorum: Deeds of the Franks.

Fiercer than any   the world has seen before.
I'll strike them down   with Durendal, my sword,
And you, companion,   strike with your own Halteclere.
We've carried them   through so many far lands,
So many battles   we've won thanks to these blades!
No evil songs   to mock them shall be made." AOI

113

The Franks can see   that hosts of Saracens
All through the field   advance on every side.
They cry out often   to Roland, Oliver,
1470   The Twelve French Peers,   to come to their defense.
Archbishop Turpin   counsels them in this way:
"Barons, my lords,   surrender not to fear,
But in God's name,   I pray you, hold your ground,
That no man mock you   in a malicious song—
Better to die   with honor on this field!
Very soon now   we'll meet our promised end;
We cannot hope   to live beyond today.
But this I tell you   is true without a doubt:
For you stand open   the gates of Paradise;
1480   You'll take your places   beside the Innocents."
Hearing these words,   the Frenchmen all rejoice;
"Montjoie!" they cry,   as with a single voice. AOI

114

From Saragossa   there came a Saracen
Who called his own   one-half of all that town.
This Climborin,   who from no knight would flee,
Heard Ganelon   swear to betray the Franks.
Kissing his mouth,   to show he held him dear,

He gave a gift: his helm with its fine stone.
Climborin says   he'll bring the Empire down,
And strike the crown   from Charlemagne's proud head.   *1490*
He rides a charger   whose name is Barbamosche—
No hawk or swallow   can fly as fast as he.
The pagan spurs,   and gives the horse his head,
Charging to strike   the Gascon Engelier.
Hauberk and shield   cannot protect him now;
Climborin's thrust   goes deep into his flesh
Until the spear-head   comes out the other side.
He flings the body   a spear's length from his horse,
And then he shouts,   "They're asking for defeat!
Strike them down, pagans—   destroy them in their ranks!" *1500*
"There died a hero.   God save us!" cry the Franks. AOI

115

And then Count Roland   calls Oliver aside:
"My lord, companion,   Engelier has been slain;
We cannot boast   a better knight than he."
The count replies,   "God grant me his revenge!"
With golden spurs   he urges on his horse,
Holding aloft   Halteclere all red with blood;
With mighty force   he strikes at Climborin,
Pulls out his sword—   the Saracen falls dead,
And demons come   to carry off his soul.   *1510*
Oliver kills   Duke Alphaïen next,
Then Escababi   is parted from his head.
The Count unhorses   seven more Arab knights
Who won't be fit   ever to fight again.
And Roland says,   "Now wrathful grows my friend!
His deeds of valor   don't shrink beside my own!
For blows like that   Charles' love is our reward."
And then he shouts,   "Strike on, you noble lords!"

116

There was a pagan   whose name was Valdabron.
1520 He raised to knighthood   the Saracen Marsile.
Four hundred galleys   he rules upon the sea,
And every sailor   is bound by oath to him.
His treachery   once took Jerusalem,
He desecrated   Solomon's Temple there—
Close to the fonts   he killed the Patriarch.
To Ganelon,   who promised him good faith,
He gave his sword   and then a thousand coins.
He rides a horse   whose name is Gramimond—
There is no falcon   who'd beat him in a race.
1530 Urging him now   with the sharp prick of spurs,
Valdabron charges Samson,   the mighty Duke;
He breaks his shield,   the hauberk splits in two,
Up to the pennon   he thrusts the spear-point through,
And fells the Duke   a spear's length from his horse:
"Strike them down, pagans,   these Franks don't have a chance!"
"There died a hero,"   say grieving men of France. AOI

117

As for Count Roland,   when he sees Samson dead,
You can imagine   the sorrow that he feels.
He spurs his horse   and charges with great speed,
1540 Holding his sword   worth more than purest gold.
Valiant, he strikes   with every ounce of strength
Valdabron's helmet,   sparkling with precious stones,
Splits his head open,   his body cased in mail;
Cleaving the saddle,   gilded and set with jewels,
The blade goes deeper   and breaks the horse's back.
Some cheer, some grieve,   but man and beast fall dead.
The pagans say,   "You've struck us a hard blow!"
And Roland answers,   "Why should I love your side?
You're in the wrong,   and you are full of pride." AOI

118

From Africa   there came an African   *1550*
Called Malquiant,   the son of King Malcud.
His arms and armor,   all overlaid with gold,
Gleam in the sunlight,   the brightest on the field.
He sits a charger   whose name is Saut-Perdu—
No horse can win   against him in a race.
Malquiant strikes   the fiery Anseïs,
Smashing to bits   the blue and crimson shield;
The hauberk breaks   where it was joined in two,
Spear-point and shaft   into the body thrust:
The Count is dead;   his time has all run through.   *1560*
The French lords say,   "Baron, we grieve for you!"

119

Now through the battle   Archbishop Turpin rides:
No tonsured priest   who ever sang a mass
Had such high courage   to do heroic deeds.
This, to the pagan: "God smite you with His curse!
You have cut down   a man my heart laments."
He sends his horse   galloping on to charge,
Strikes Malquiant   through his Toledo shield,
And flings his body   onto the grassy field.

120

And then comes forward   a pagan called Grandoine,   *1570*
Capuel's son,   he's Cappadocia's heir.
He sits a horse   whose name is Marmorie—
It gallops faster   than any bird can fly.
He loosens reins   and pricks him with his spurs
To charge Count Gerin   with all his skill and force.
The crimson shield   falls from the Frenchman's neck,

His hauberk breaks,   most of it splits away,
Then the blue banner   thrusts deep into his flesh,
And Grandoine hurls   his body to a rock.
1580 That pagan kills   Gerin's friend Gerier,
And Berenger,   and Gui of Saint-Antoine;
He charges next   the mighty Duke Austorge,
Lord of Valence   and Envers on the Rhône,
Who falls down dead   as all the pagans cheer.
The Frenchmen say,   "Our end is coming near."

121

Roland holds high   his sword stained red with blood.
He has not missed   the outcry of the Franks,
And feels such sorrow   he thinks his heart will break.
This, to the pagan: "God's curse upon you fall!
1590 I'll sell you dear   the noble lord you've slain!"
He spurs his horse   who cares not to delay,
Seeks out Grandoine,   hoping to make him pay.

122

Grandoine is valiant,   powerful, very brave;
He is a hero,   bold on the battlefield.
All of a sudden   Count Roland bars his path.
Although the pagan   never saw him before,
By his proud face   he knows him, by his eyes,
His noble bearing,   his stature, tall and strong;
Grandoine can't help   but tremble with great fear.
1600 He tries to flee,   but cannot get away
Before Count Roland   stops him with such a blow
That his whole helmet   down to the nose-piece breaks,
The sword blade cleaves   through nose and mouth and teeth,
Down through his body   encased in shining mail,
Into the saddle   all silver-trimmed and gold,

And drives on deep   into the horse's back.
Nothing can save them—   both man and beast fall dead.
Spaniards cry out   in horror at the sight.
The Frenchmen say,   "Our lord knows how to fight!"

123

The wondrous battle   is spirited and grim;   *1610*
Blow after blow   the angry Frenchmen strike.
Their sword blades cleave   through fists and ribs and spines,
Through cloth and armor   into the living flesh.
On the green grass,   the bright blood flows in streams.
The pagans say,   "This is too much for us!
Mohammed's curse   upon the Empire fall!
There are no men   as hard to kill as these."
And to Marsile   the Saracens cry out:
"Ride to our aid,   or we'll be put to rout!"

124

The battle grows   ever more swift and fierce.   *1620*
The Frenchmen strike   keen blows with burnished spears.
You would have seen   so many in great pain,
So many dead,   so many drenched in blood!
Face up or downward,   one on the other lies.
The Saracens   cannot bear any more:
They flee the field,   whether they will or no.
The wrathful Franks   pursue them as they go. AOI

125

King Marsile sees   the slaughter of his men.
Then horns and trumpets   ring out at his command,
And he rides on   with his assembled host.   *1630*

One Saracen   rides out in front: Abisme,
The fiercest man   in all that company.
Evil at heart,   and guilty of great crimes,
He has no faith   in Mary's holy Son.
This pagan's skin   is black as melted pitch.
He'd rather murder   or do vile treachery
Than have the gift   of all Galicia's gold.
He never laughs   or joins in any sport,
But he is bold   and valiant when he fights.
1640   This makes him dear   to the foul King Marsile;
He bears the Dragon,   flag of the Saracens.
Archbishop Turpin   will be no friend to him—
Seeing this pagan,   he longs to strike him down.
In a low voice   he speaks thus to himself:
"This man must be   a mighty heretic—
Surely his death   has been too long delayed.
I have no love   for men who are afraid."

126

And so the battle   begins with Turpin's charge.
He rides a horse   he took from King Grossaille,
1650   That time in Denmark   he fought him to his death.
The horse is swift   and spirited and proud;
He has arched hooves,   powerful, slender legs;
His haunches short,   his quarters large around.
Deep is his chest,   his back set straight and high.
His tail is white,   yellow his flowing mane,
His ears are small,   his head of tawny gold;
No charger set   to race him has a chance.
Archbishop Turpin   spurs on against Abisme—
And with what valor!   Nothing can stop him now.
1660   He strikes the shield   a superhuman blow;

1647. That is, "I never loved a coward or cowardice"; but it seems clear that
Turpin refers to himself, feeling perhaps even a bit reluctant to attack so dreadful a Saracen.

Its surface sparkles   with topaz, amethyst,
Stones of great virtue,   rubies that hotly glow—
(A devil's gift   to the Emir Galafre
In Val Metas;   he gave it to Abisme.)
But Turpin's spear   accords it no respect:
After his blow   it isn't worth a cent.
Right through that pagan   his spear thrusts like a spit;
He throws the body   into an empty space.
The Frenchmen say,   "Against him no one stands!
The holy staff   is safe in Turpin's hands."   *1670*

127

Count Roland says   to Oliver his friend:
"My lord companion,   I'm sure you will agree
That our Archbishop   makes a most valiant knight—
There is none better   on earth beneath the sky;
With lance in hand,   or spear, how he can fight!"
The Count replies,   "Then let's go to his side!"
When he has spoken,   the Franks attack once more.
Hard are the blows,   the fighting pitiless;
Grievous the loss   of valiant Christian men.
Then to behold   Roland and Oliver   *1680*
Wielding their swords   to cut the pagans down!
Beside them Turpin   thrusts with his mighty spear.
We know what happened   according to the *Geste*,
Chronicles, records   bear witness to the fact:
Four thousand pagans   by those few Franks were slain.
Through four assaults   the Frenchmen hold their ground.
But with the fifth   their strength comes to an end.
That final charge   kills all the knights of France
Except for sixty   who by God's will survive—
They'll make the pagans   pay dearly for their lives! AOI   *1690*

1662. "Stones of great virtue" comes from a suggestion of Jenkins regarding *esterminals*.

128

Count Roland sees   the slaughter of the Franks.
He says these words   to Oliver his friend:
"Noble companion,   how does it look to you?
So many Franks   lie dead upon the field—
Well could we weep   for that fair land, sweet France,
Which will not see   these valiant lords again.
Oh! Charles, my friend,   if only you were here!
Oliver, brother,   how can we call him back?
Is there no way   for us to send him word?"
1700   Oliver answers,   "No, I do not know how.
Better to die   than lose our honor now." AOI

129

Then Roland says,   "I'll sound the Oliphant.
King Charles will hear it   on the high mountain pass;
I promise you,   the Franks will all turn back."
Oliver answers,   "Then you would bring disgrace
And such dishonor   on your whole family
The shame of it   would last them all their lives.
Three times I asked,   and you would not agree;
You still can do it,   but not with my consent.
1710   To sound the horn   denies your valor now.
And both your arms   are red with blood of foes!"
The Count replies,   "I've struck some pretty blows." AOI

130

Then Roland says,   "This is a heavy fight.
I'll blow my horn,   and Charlemagne will hear."
Oliver says,   "Then you'll disgrace your name.
Each time I asked you,   companion, you refused.

1699. Manderum nuveles: Roland wants Charles, above all, to *know*.

If Charles were with us,   we would not come to grief.
No one can say   our Franks have been to blame.
I promise you—   I swear it by my beard—
If I should live   to see my sister's face,   *1720*
You'll never lie   in Aude's sweet embrace!" AOI

131

Then says the Count,   "You're angry at me. Why?"
Oliver answers,   "Roland, you are to blame.
Allied with reason,   courage is not unwise;
Men of good sense   do more for us than fools.
You were reckless,   and so these Franks have died.
Never again   will we serve Charlemagne.
Had you believed me,   my lord would be here now,
We would have fought   and beat the Saracens,
Marsile would be   our prisoner, or dead.   *1730*
We are the victims   of your great prowess now!
We won't be there,   alas! to help King Charles,
A man whose peer   will not be seen on earth.
And you will die,   leaving sweet France to shame.
Brothers-in-arms   we've been until this day;
Now we have only   a last farewell to say." AOI

132

Archbishop Turpin,   hearing the angry words,
Urges his horse   with spurs made of pure gold,
And riding up,   reproaches both of them:

1731. *Vostre proëcce, Rollant, mar la veïmes!* The use of *mar* in this sense, it
seems to me, should not be translated so as to imply an absolute condemnation.
Oliver, even in fury, would hardly regret the whole experience of Roland's valor,
but rather would lament that so much valor should come to so unfortunate an
end (similarly, line 1860). The same considerations apply when *mar* is used
with *estre*, as in *Barun, tant mare fus!* (line 1604), or *Tant mar fustes hardiz!*
(line 2027).

1740   "Roland, my lord,   and you, Lord Oliver,
        End your dispute,   I pray you, in God's name.
        It's too late now   to blow the horn for help,
        But just the same,   that's what you'd better do.
        If the King comes,   at least we'll be avenged—
        Why should the Spaniards   go home safe to rejoice?
        And then the Franks   will ride back to this place;
        They'll find us dead,   our bodies hacked by swords,
        Put us in coffins   carried on horses' backs,
        And they will weep   for pity and for grief.
1750   We will be buried   with honor in a church,
        And not be eaten   by wolves and pigs and dogs."
        Then Roland answers: "Your words are true, my lord."

133

        Count Roland presses   the horn against his mouth;
        He grasps it hard,   and sounds a mighty blast.
        High are the hills,   that great voice reaches far—
        They hear it echo   full thirty leagues around.
        Charlemagne hears,   and so do all his men.
        The Emperor says,   "Our Franks are in a fight!"
        Count Ganelon   returns a swift reply:
1760   "Except from you,   I'd take that for a lie!" AOI

134

        And now Count Roland,   in anguish and in pain,
        With all his strength   sounds the great horn again.
        A fountain of bright blood   leaps from his mouth;
        His brain is bursting   against his forehead's bone.
        That mighty voice   cries out a second time;
        Charlemagne hears it,   high on the mountain pass,
        Duke Naimon listens,   and so do all the Franks.
        Then says the King,   "That is Count Roland's horn!

He'd never sound it,   except for an attack."
Ganelon says,   "What battle can there be?   *1770*
You have grown old,   your hair is streaked with white;
The words you speak   could well befit a child.
You ought to know   how great is Roland's pride—
The wonder is   God suffers it so long.
He captured Noples,   and not by your command,
And then flushed out   the Saracens inside;
He fought them all,   Roland, your loyal man,
And then took water   and washed the field of blood,
Hoping that you   would not detect the fight.
Just for a rabbit   he'll blow his horn all day!   *1780*
He's only boasting   how he'll outdo his peers.
No one on earth   would meet him in the field!
Ride on, I tell you!   What are we waiting for?
We've far to go   to see our lands once more." AOI

135

Blood is flowing   over Count Roland's mouth;
His brain has broken   right through his forehead's bone.
He sounds the horn   in anguish and in pain.
Charlemagne hears,   and so do all the Franks.
Then says the King,   "How long that horn resounds!"
Duke Naimon answers,   "Great valor swells the sound!   *1790*
Roland is fighting: he must have been betrayed—
And by that man   who tells you to hang back.
Take up your arms,   let your war-cry ring out!
Your household needs you,   now speed to its defense.
You've heard enough   how Roland's horn laments!"

1778. Brault (pp. 216-218) indicates that the fantastic "field washing" may be
the effect of difficulty in reading the line; the reference may be to the washing of
blood from a sword. He suggests that Charles would have been hearing the story
for the first time, but, if so, this would refer only to the details of the event,
since the conquest of Noples is the first that Roland mentions in his speech
against Marsile (198).

136

The Emperor Charles   orders his horns to sound.
The French dismount,   prepare themselves for war.
They put on hauberks,   helmets and golden swords;
Their shields are good,   heavy their spears and strong,
1800 Their battle-flags   are crimson, blue and white.
Riding their chargers,   the barons of the host
Spur on and gallop   back through the mountain pass.
Each to the other   pronounces this same vow:
"When we get there,   if Roland's still alive,
We'll fight beside him,   striking hard blows and straight."
What does it matter?   Their help will come too late.

137

All afternoon   the sun shines bright and clear,
Armor and weapons   are gleaming in the light,
Hauberks and helmets   glitter as if on fire,
1810 And all the shields,   brilliant with painted flowers,
And all the spears   and gilded battle-flags.
In bitter wrath   the Emperor rides on,
The men of France   in sorrow and in rage.
There is not one   who can hold back his tears;
Because of Roland,   the Frenchmen are afraid.
King Charles commands   that Ganelon be seized;
Summoning forth   all of his household cooks,
He tells their chief,   Besgon, what should be done:
"Here is a felon   I'm leaving in your charge—
1820 He has betrayed   the vassals of my house."
The cook takes over;   a hundred kitchen boys,
The best and worst,   will guard Count Ganelon.
They pluck the hairs   from his moustache and beard,
Each with his fist   strikes him four mighty blows,
And then they beat him   with heavy sticks and clubs.

An iron collar   is put around his neck,
And then they chain him   as if he were a bear.
On a mule's back,   trussed up, he will remain.
They'll guard him well,   and wait for Charlemagne. AOI

138

High are the hills,   and shadowy and vast,   *1830*
Deep the ravines,   and swift the mountain streams.
The trumpets sound   ahead and to the rear,
Blaring replies   to Roland's Oliphant.
In bitter wrath   the Emperor rides on,
The men of France   in sorrow and in rage;
Not one but grieves   and bitterly laments,
Praying that God   will keep Count Roland safe
Until they come   and join him in the field—
How they will fight   when they are at his side!
What does it matter   how loyally they strive?   *1840*
They'll be too late   whenever they arrive. AOI

139

Now Charlemagne   rides on in his great rage;
His beard, defiant,   outside his hauberk lies.
The lords of France   spur for the utmost speed,
There isn't one   but angrily laments
That they can't be   already on the field
Where Roland fights   against the Saracens.
I think his wound   won't let him long survive,
But God! the sixty   still fighting at his side—
No king or chieftain   has ever had their like. AOI   *1850*

1846. Rollant le cataigne: the term refers to a military leader, but it is not as
precise as "captain."

140

Count Roland looks at   the mountains and the hills
Where all around him   the Franks are lying dead;
He weeps for them,   as a true knight would do.
"Barons, my lords,   may God forgive your sins,
And grant your souls   a place in Paradise;
On holy flowers   may you forever rest!
I've never seen   vassals better than you;
You followed me   so loyally and long,
For Charlemagne   we've won such mighty lands!
1860   The King's own household,   alas! brings him to woe.
And that fair country   where it is sweet to live
Today laid waste   and cruelly bereaved!
Barons of France,   because of me you die;
I can't protect you,   I cannot keep you safe:
Look now to God   who never told a lie.
Oliver, brother,   faithful I'll be to you;
I'll die of grief,   if not by pagan spears.
My lord, companion,   there's still work for us here!"

1863. The crucial words *pur mei* must certainly be understood as "because of me" rather than "for my sake," which would be not only presumptuous but inaccurate. A correct translation here, however important, is still ambiguous: Jenkins translates "because of me," but understands it to mean "through my fault." "For my sake" is also open to multiple interpretations: Brault translates *pur mei* this way, but, according to his commentary, would have it refer only to Roland's gratitude and sorrow. The translations of Sayers and Merwin also read "for my sake," no doubt for different reasons. Bédier has *pour moi*, Goldin "for me." At least as far as the surface equivalence is concerned, line 1090, *Que ja pur mei perdet sa valur France!* (I won't betray   the glory of sweet France!) offers a particularly clear example of *pur mei* meaning "because of me" and not possibly "for my sake" or "for me."

1866. The literal meaning is clear: Oliver, brother, you I must not fail. There is no way to know which part, if any, of the speech was spoken aloud; Oliver does seem to have been present. Goldin underlines "you" in his translation, and, although there has not been as much commentary on this line as on the earlier part of the *laisse,* the tendency has been to understand that Roland did break faith with others. Equally grammatical, however, would be a reading in which "must" and "must not" were contrasted; Roland, by the nature of his commit-

141

Roland has gone   back to the battlefield.
With Durendal   he strikes heroic blows: *1870*
Faldrun of Pui   he cuts down first of all,
Then twenty-four   of the best pagan knights.
No man has ever   wanted revenge so much.
Just as the stag   runs to escape the hounds,
So do the pagans   before Count Roland flee.
Says the Archbishop,   "Bravely you fight, and well!
Yours is the spirit   a chevalier must have,
If he bears arms   and has a horse to ride:
A man in battle   ought to be fierce and strong—
For one who isn't,   I wouldn't give two cents.   *1880*
Instead of fighting   let him become a monk
And spend his days   praying for all our sins."
Roland replies,   "Strike on, and spare not one!"
With that the Franks   begin to fight once more.
Many a Christian   falls to the pagan swords.

142

A man who knows   all captives will be slain
In such a battle   fights to the end of strength;

---

ment, *had* to fail the Franks, that is, could not prevent their deaths, could not
fulfill their expectations. He still can hope not to "fail" Oliver, which, since there
was no way to protect him, probably refers to their mutual loyalty. Punctuation
between this line and the following varies with the editor, but the mere juxta-
position makes a connection. It is possible that in this moment when absolute
and relative viewpoints have come together for Roland, what he means by not
failing Oliver is to die of grief, or simply not to survive Roncevaux.

1881-2. Tavernier and Jenkins believe that this passage does not necessarily
imply that cloistered monks are inferior to good knights. Such an interpretation
would seem to me possible only if one considered that in the heat of battle
Turpin spoke more emphatically than he normally would in describing the cate-
gories of worthy activities.

And so the Franks   like lions face their foes.
Behold Marsile: as a true knight would do,
1890   He sits the horse   that he has named Gaignon,
Pricks with sharp spurs,   and rides against Bevon,
The lord of Beaune   and also of Dijon.
He breaks his shield,   the hauberk splits in two—
With that one blow   he fells the Frenchman dead.
Then Marsile kills   Ivoire and Ivon too,
And with them dies   Gérard of Roussillon.
Seeing that, Roland,   who isn't far away,
Says to the pagan,   "God smite you with His curse!
To you I owe   these good companions slain—
1900   Nor shall we part   before that debt is paid!
Now is the time   to teach you my sword's name."
With that he charges   as a true knight would do;
The Count's keen sword   cuts off Marsile's right hand.
Then Jurfaleu   surrenders his blond head—
He was a Prince,   the son of King Marsile.
The pagans cry,   "Mohammed help us now!
Gods of our country,   give us revenge on Charles,
For he has sent   such felons here to fight
That death itself   can't drive them from the field."
1910   They tell each other,   "Let's get away from here!"
A hundred thousand   run from the French attack;
Whoever calls,   they won't be coming back.

143

What does it matter   that King Marsile has fled?
They still must fight   his uncle the Caliph,
The lord of Carthage,   Alfrere, and Garmalie,
That land accursed   called Ethiopia
Whose black men serve   as the Caliph commands.
They have big noses,   their ears stick out too far;
Some fifty thousand   have come to fight the Franks.

1890. Marsile's horse is called Watchdog.

They gallop boldly,   and in wild fury charge,   *1920*
Shouting the war-cry   dear to the pagan hosts.
Then Roland says,   "Here we'll win martyrdom.
Now I can see   how little time is left;
But cursed be he   who lets his life go cheap!
Strike them, my lords,   strike with your shining swords!
Give them a battle   whether you live or die,
That none may say   we brought sweet France to shame.
When Charlemagne   comes to this battlefield,
He'll see the hosts   of slaughtered Saracens—
For each of us   some fifteen pagans dead;   *1930*
Charles won't reproach us,   he'll bless us all instead." AOI

144

When Roland sees   this horde of infidels
Who all are darker   than is the blackest ink,
With nothing white   except their gleaming teeth,
He says aloud,   "There isn't any doubt,
Today we'll die—   I can believe it now.
Follow me, Frenchmen!   We'll give them one more charge!"
Oliver says,   "The devil take the last!"
The French attack;   their blows fall hard and fast.

145

And when the pagans   see how few Franks are left,   *1940*
They take much pride   and comfort from the fact,
Telling each other,   "King Charles is in the wrong."
Then the Caliph,   astride a sorrel horse,
Pricks with gold spurs   and gallops from behind
To land his spear   deep in Oliver's back.
The gleaming hauberk   shatters and splits away,
The spear goes through   and opens up his chest.
Says the Caliph,   "You've taken a hard blow!
Charlemagne left you   to wait here for your doom.

1950   Let him not glory   in what he's done to Spain—
Your death alone   avenges all our slain."

146

Oliver feels   how close he is to death.
He raises high   Halteclere's bright burnished blade,
Strikes the Caliph,   and splits his tall gold helm,
Its jewels and flowers   fall shattered to the ground;
He cleaves his head   right down into the teeth,
Wrenching the sword,   he hurls the body down.
Then says the Count,   "Be damned, you Saracen!
Whatever Charles   may have lost here today,
1960   At least I'm sure   no wife or lady friend
Will hear you boasting,   safe in your lands again,
Of how you captured   silver or gold from me:
You'll have no triumph   to take home and parade!"
And then he calls   Count Roland to his aid. AOI

147

Oliver knows   he has a fatal wound.
He longs for vengeance—   he'll never have enough.
In the melee   he fights on valiantly,
He cuts through spears,   the pagans' studded shields,
And feet and fists   and saddle-trees and spines.
1970   Whoever watched him   cut pagans limb from limb,
Bodies piled up   around him on the ground,
Would know that once   he'd seen a noble lord.
The Count remembers   the war-cry of King Charles,
And loud and clear   his voice rings out, "Montjoie!"
He calls to Roland,   summons his friend and peer,

1951. The one truly noteworthy compliment to Oliver in the poem comes from
a distinguished pagan.

"My lord, companion,   come fight beside me now!
We'll part in sorrow   before the sun goes down." AOI

148

Roland is there;   he sees Oliver's face,
The skin is ashen,   so pallid it looks grey,
And from his wounds   bright blood is spurting out;   *1980*
Its heavy drops   flow down him to the ground.
"O God!" says Roland,   "I don't know what to do.
Was such great valor   destined to be cut down!
My noble friend,   you'll have no peer on earth.
Alas, sweet France!   Now you have fallen low,
Bereft of vassals,   so many valiant men;
The Emperor Charles   will sorely feel the lack."
With these words Roland   faints on his horse's back. AOI

149

Here is Count Roland   unconscious on his horse;
Oliver, wounded   and very close to death,   *1990*
Has bled so much   that both his eyes are dimmed:
Now far or near   he can't see well enough
To give a name   to any man alive.
When he encounters   Count Roland in the field,
Oliver strikes him,   cleaving his golden helm
Brilliant with jewels—   the nose-piece cracks in two—
And yet the blade   does not touch face or head.
Roland's eyes open,   and looking at his friend,
Softly and gently   he asks him only this:
"My lord, companion,   it's Roland—did you know?   *2000*
I've always loved you;   did you intend that blow?
You gave no challenge   before you charged at me."
Oliver says,   "I recognize your voice,
But I can't see you—   God keep you in His sight!

I struck at you!   I pray you, pardon me."
Roland replies,   "I am not hurt at all;
I do forgive you,   here and in front of God."
When he had spoken,   each leaned down toward his friend.
So, with great love,   they parted in the end.

150

2010   Oliver suffers   the agonies of death;
He feels his eyes   turn back into his head,
He cannot hear,   he cannot see at all.
Now he dismounts,   and lying on the ground,
Aloud he asks   forgiveness for his sins;
He clasps his hands,   and holds them toward the sky,
Praying that God   will grant him Paradise,
And give His blessing   to Charles and to sweet France,
And to Count Roland   above all other men.
Then his heart fails him,   his shining helmet bows.
2020   All of his body   sinks down against the ground;
The Count is dead—   no longer did he stay.
Lord Roland weeps,   lamenting bitterly;
Many have grieved,   but no man more than he.

151

When Roland sees   that Oliver is dead,
Lying face downward,   stretched out against the ground,
With tender words   he bids his friend farewell:
"Alas, companion!   Your valor ends in woe.
We were together   so many years and days;
Never did you harm me,   nor I hurt you.
2030   Now you are dead,   I grieve to be alive."
The Marquis faints   just as he says these words,

2031. A *marchis* is the lord of a march, or border territory. The only information Einhard gives about Roland is that he was Count of the March of Brittany.

Still on his horse,   whose name is Veillantif;
The fine gold stirrups   will keep him sitting straight,
So he won't fall   however he may sway.

152

Before Count Roland   recovers from his faint,
While he still sits   unconscious on his horse,
The battle brings   disaster to his men:
The Franks are dead—   he's lost them, every one
Save the Archbishop   and Gautier de l'Hum
Who, from the mountain,   has now returned at last.   *2040*
He fought a battle   with Spanish Saracens.
His men are dead;   their enemies have won.
Down toward the valleys,   he flees now, all alone,
Searching for Roland,   calling to him for help:
"Ah, noble Count!   Where are you, valiant lord?
When you were with me,   I never was afraid.
It's Gautier—   I conquered Maelgut!
Droon is my uncle,   his aged head is grey.
You used to love me,   because you knew me brave.
My spear is broken,   my shield has been pierced through,   *2050*
My hauberk's links   scattered and snapped apart,
Deep in my body   a pagan lance has thrust;
I'm dying now,   but they have bought me dear."
Roland wakes up   to hear his final words;
Turning his horse,   toward Gautier he spurs. AOI

153

Count Roland, grieving   and filled with bitter rage,
Rides once again   through the thick of the fight.
Twenty Spaniards   he throws dead to the ground,
Gautier kills six,   Archbishop Turpin five.
The pagans say,   "These men are monstrous fierce!   *2060*

Take care, my lords,   don't let them get away.
If you aren't traitors,   you'll rush upon them now—
If you aren't cowards,   they won't escape alive!"
Then riding onward   with a great hue and cry,
They charge the Franks   once more from every side. AOI

154

There is Count Roland,   a noble warrior,
Gautier de l'Hum,   a worthy chevalier,
Archbishop Turpin,   a veteran and brave:
None would be willing   to fail the other two.
2070   In the melee   they strike the pagans down.
A thousand Spaniards   dismount to fight on foot,
While forty thousand   stay on their horses' backs—
And even so   they don't dare come too near.
They throw their lances,   hurl their keen-bladed spears,
All sorts of weapons   come flying at the Franks;
With the first blows,   Count Gautier is killed,
Turpin of Reims   soon finds his shield pierced through,
His helmet breaks—   he's wounded in the head—
His chain-mail hauberk   is cracked and splits apart,
2080   Four pagan spears   strike deep into his flesh,
His war-horse, dying,   carries him to the ground.
O God! What sorrow   to see Turpin go down! AOI

155

Turpin of Reims,   finding himself unhorsed,
With four deep wounds   where spears thrust through his flesh,
Leaps up again,   great fighter that he is,
Looks for Count Roland,   and hastens to his side,
Saying just this: "I am not beaten yet!
No man of courage   gives up while he's alive."

He draws Almace   whose blade is burnished steel,
Strikes in the throng   a thousand blows and more.   *2090*
Soon Charles will say   that Turpin spared no foe:
They found four hundred   around him in the field,
Some of them wounded,   some of them thrust clean through,
And there were others   who parted with their heads.
So says the *Geste,*   and someone who was there:
Saint Giles for whom   Our Lord works miracles
Left an account   in Laon's church in France;
Everyone knows this,   or nothing understands.

156

Roland delivers   many a skillful blow,
But now his body   is fevered, drenched with sweat,   *2100*
His head is throbbing;   he is in dreadful pain,
His temples broken   from sounding his great horn.
Longing to know   if Charles is on his way,
Weakly, once more,   he blows the Oliphant.
King Charles stands still,   listening to that call;
"My lords," he says,   "now we have come to woe!
My nephew Roland   takes leave of us this day—
His horn's voice tells me   he won't be long alive.
Who wants to be there   had better speed his horse.
Let every trumpet   the host commands resound!"   *2110*
And sixty thousand   rang from the lofty peaks
Down through the valleys,   echoing loud and clear.
The pagans, listening,   think it no empty boast—
They say, "Here come   King Charles and all his host." AOI

157

The pagans say,   "Now Charles is coming back.
Those trumpet calls   rally the men of France;

We'll have great losses   if the Emperor comes,
And if Count Roland   lives to make war again,
We may as well   surrender all of Spain."
2120   About four hundred   assemble, helmeted,
The best who fought   among the Saracens;
With all their might   these men attack anew,
And then Count Roland   has work enough to do. AOI

158

When Roland sees   the pagans closing in,
His heart grows stronger,   and prouder and more fierce.
He'll yield to none,   as long as he's alive.
Astride the horse   whose name is Veillantif,
He gallops toward them,   pricking with golden spurs;
Into the throng   he charges to attack.
2130   Archbishop Turpin   is fighting at his side.
The pagans say,   "Let's get away from here!
Those trumpet calls   mean that the Franks are near—
Their mighty King,   great Charles, will soon appear!'

159

Count Roland's friendship   no coward ever knew,
Nor any man   false-hearted or too proud,
Nor any knight   who was not skilled at war.
To the Archbishop   Roland addressed these words:
"I am on horseback,   my lord, and you're on foot;
For love of you,   here I shall take my stand—
2140   We'll meet together   what good or evil comes,
No mortal man   will make me leave your side.
We'll teach the pagans   here on the field today
To name our swords: Almace and Durendal!"
Turpin replies,   "Curse him whose arm grows slack!
We'll be avenged   when Charlemagne comes back."

160

The pagans say,   "Ours were unlucky stars!
Would that this evil day   had never dawned!
We've lost our Peers,   our lords have all been slain,
The valiant Charles   is coming back again.
Now we can hear   the trumpets of his host,   *2150*
The mighty clamor   when the Franks shout 'Montjoie!'
And this Count Roland   is hideously fierce—
He can't be conquered   by men of flesh and blood.
Let's cast our lances   and then leave him alone."
The Saracens   throw many javelins,
Lances and darts,   and feathered throwing spears.
Count Roland's shield   is broken and pierced through,
His hauberk's mail   is cracked and split apart,
And still his body   has not been touched at all.
But Veillantif   has suffered thirty wounds;   *2160*
Beneath Count Roland   he falls dead to the ground.
Then all the pagans   yield to their fear and flee;
And Roland stands,   dismounted, on the field. AOI

161

The pagans flee,   furious and enraged,
Trying their best   to get away in Spain.
Count Roland lacks the means   to chase them now,
For he has lost   his war-horse Veillantif;
Against his will   he has to go on foot.
He went to give   Archbishop Turpin help,
Unlaced his helmet,   removed it from his head,   *2170*
And then took off   the hauberk of light mail;
The under-tunic   he cut into long strips
With which he stanched   the largest of his wounds.
Then, lifting Turpin,   carried him in his arms
To soft green grass,   and gently laid him down.
In a low voice   Roland made this request:

"My noble lord,   I pray you, give me leave,
For our companions,   the men we held so dear,
Must not be left   abandoned now in death.
2180   I want to go   and seek out every one,
Carry them here,   and place them at your feet."
Said the Archbishop,   "I grant it willingly.
The field belongs,   thank God, to you and me."

162

Alone, Count Roland   walks through the battlefield,
Searching the valleys,   searching the mountain heights.
Gerin he found,   and Gerier his friend,
He found Aton   and then Count Berenger,
Proud Anseïs he found,   and then Samson,
Gérard the Old,   the Count of Roussillon.
2190   He took these barons,   and carried every one
Back to the place   where the Archbishop was,
And then he put them   in ranks at Turpin's knees.
Seeing them, Turpin   cannot restrain his tears;
Raising his hand,   he blesses all the dead.
And then he says,   "You've come to grief, my lords!
May God in His glory   receive your souls,
Among bright flowers   set you in Paradise!
Now I must die,   in anguish and in pain;
Never again   will I see Charlemagne."

163

2200   Roland goes back   to search the field once more,
And his companion   he finds there, Oliver.
Lifting him in his arms,   he holds him close,

2183. The Archbishop's statement confirms the fact that the Battle of Roncevaux was a French *victory*.

Brings him to Turpin   as quickly as he can,
Beside the others   places him on a shield;
Turpin absolves him,   signing him with the cross,
And then they yield   to pity and to grief.
Count Roland says,   "Brother-in-arms, fair friend,
You were the son   of Renier, the Duke
Who held the land   where Runers valley lies.
For breaking lances,   for shattering thick shields,   *2210*
Bringing the proud   to terror and defeat,
Giving the worthy   protection and advice,
Crushing vile pagans,   who cannot see the light,
In all the world   there is no better knight."

164

When Roland sees   that all his peers are dead,
And Oliver   whom he so dearly loved,
He feels such sorrow   that he begins to weep;
Drained of all color,   his face turns ashen pale,
His grief is more   than any man could bear,
He falls down, fainting   whether he will or no.   *2220*
Says the Archbishop,   "Baron, you've come to woe."

165

When the Archbishop   sees Roland on the ground,
He feels more sorrow   than he has ever known.
He reaches out   to grasp the Oliphant;
A swift stream waters   the plain at Roncevaux,
And there, for Roland,   he wants to fill the horn.
Taking short steps,   staggering, he sets out,
But in his weakness   he can't go very far—
He has no strength,   his wounds have bled too much;
Before a man   could walk a hundred feet   *2230*
Turpin has fallen—   his noble heart has failed.
He feels death's power   beginning to prevail.

166

Meanwhile Count Roland   recovers from his faint,
He rises to his feet,   but in great pain.
He looks around him,   he searches up and down;
Beyond the place   where his companions lie,
Prone on the grass,   he sees the noble lord,
Archbishop Turpin,   God's delegate on earth.
Count Roland hears him   confessing he has sinned,
2240 With his clasped hands   held upward toward the sky,
Praying that God   will give him Paradise.
Turpin is dead   who fought for Charlemagne.
With mighty blows,   with wise and holy words,
Against the pagans   he championed the Faith.
May God in heaven   bless him and grant him grace.

167

Roland sees Turpin   lying there on the ground,
Entrails protruding   from his enormous wounds;
Above his forehead   his brains are bubbling out.
On Turpin's chest,   between his collarbones,
2250 Roland has crossed   the beautiful white hands.
Now he laments   as it is done in France:
"O nobly born,   illustrious chevalier,
To heaven's glory   I now commend your soul;
Our Lord will never   be served more willingly.
Since the Apostles,   there has been none like you
To keep the Law,   and bring men to the Faith.
From pain and sorrow   may your free soul arise;
May you find open   the gates of Paradise!"

168

Now Roland knows   that death is very near.
2260 His ears give way,   he feels his brains gush out.

He prays that God   will summon all his peers;
Then, for himself,   he prays to Gabriel.
Taking the horn,   to keep it from all shame,
With Durendal   clasped in his other hand,
He goes on, farther   than a good cross-bow shot,
West into Spain,   crossing a fallow field.
Up on a hilltop,   under two lofty trees,
Four marble blocks   are standing on the grass.
But when he comes there,   Count Roland faints once more,
He falls down backward;   now he is at death's door.   *2270*

169

High are the hills   and very tall the trees,
The four great blocks   of polished marble shine;
On the green grass   the Count is lying still.
A Saracen   watches with steady eyes:
This man feigned death,   hiding among the slain;
His face and body   he had besmeared with blood.
Now he stands up   and dashes forward fast—
He's handsome, strong   and very valiant too,
But he won't live   to profit from his pride;
He falls on Roland,   wanting to have his arms,   *2280*
And says these words: "Charles' nephew lost the fight!
When I go home,   his sword shall be my prize."
But as he pulls it,   Roland comes back to life.

170

Count Roland feels   the pagan take his sword,
And opening his eyes,   he says just this:
"You look to me   like no one on our side!"
Raising the horn   he'd wanted to keep safe,
He strikes the helmet   shining with gold and jewels,
Shatters the steel,   smashes the skull and bones;
He puts both eyes   out of the pagan's head,   *2290*

And sends his body   crashing against the ground.
And then he asks him,   "How did you get so brave,
Dog, to attack me   with or without just cause?
Whoever heard this   would say you were insane!
But I have cracked   the Oliphant's broad bell;
Its gold and crystals   were shattered as it fell."

171

Now Roland feels   that he is going blind.
The Count stands upright,   using what strength remains;
All of the color   has vanished from his face.
2300   In front of him   there is a dark grey stone.
He strikes ten blows   in bitterness and grief;
The steel blade grates   but will not break or dent.
Then Roland cries,   "O Holy Mary, help!
O Durendal,   alas for your fair fame!
My life is over,   you won't be in my care.
We've won such battles   together in the field,
So many lands   we've conquered, you and I,
For Charles to rule   whose beard is silver-grey.
No man must have you   who fights and runs away!
2310   You have been long   in a good vassal's hands;
You'll have no equal   in all of holy France."

172

Count Roland strikes   the hard sardonyx stone;
The steel blade grates   but will not chip or break.
When Roland sees   he can't destroy his sword,
Then, to himself,   grieving, he speaks its praise:
"O Durendal,   how fair you are, and bright!
Against the sunlight   your keen steel gleams and flames!
Charles was that time   in Moriane's Vales
When, by God's will,   an angel from the sky

Said to bestow you   upon a chieftain Count: *2320*
The noble King   girded you at my side.
With you I won him   Anjou and Brittany,
Conquered Poitou   and after that all Maine,
With you I won him   that free land, Normandy,
Conquered Provence,   and then all Aquitaine,
And Lombardy,   Romagna after that.
With you I won him   Bavaria, Flanders,
Bulgaria   and all of Poland too;
Constantinople   paid homage to King Charles,
In Saxony   he does as he desires.   *2330*
With you I conquered   the Irish and the Scots,
And England too   the King holds as his own.
So many countries   we've won him, many lands
Ruled by King Charles   whose flowing beard is white.
For your sake now   I suffer grief and pain—
Better to die   than leave you here in Spain.
Almighty Father,   keep sweet France from that shame!"

173

Count Roland strikes   against a dark grey stone;
More of it falls   than I can make you see.
The steel blade grates   but will not crack or break;   *2340*
Against the sky   it springs back up again.
Count Roland knows   he can't destroy his sword.
Then, to himself,   he quietly laments:
"O Durendal,   holy you are, and fair!
You have great relics   within your hilt of gold:
Saint Peter's tooth,   drops of Saint Basil's blood,
Hairs from the head   of my lord Saint Denis,
Part of a garment   that Holy Mary wore—
For any pagan   to hold you would be wrong;
Only by Christians   can you be rightly served.   *2350*
May you not fall   into a coward's hands!
Many wide lands   we've conquered, you and I,

For Charles to rule   whose flowing beard is white;
They have increased   his majesty and might."

174

Count Roland feels   the very grip of death
Which from his head   is reaching for his heart.
He hurries then   to go beneath a pine;
In the green grass   he lies down on his face,
Placing beneath him   the sword and Oliphant;
2360   He turns his head   to look toward pagan Spain.
He does these things   in order to be sure
King Charles will say,   and with him all the Franks,
The noble Count   conquered until he died.
He makes confession,   for all his sins laments,
Offers his glove   to God in penitence. AOI

175

Now Roland feels   his time has all run out.
He looks toward Spain   from high on a steep hill,
And, with one hand   beating his breast, he says:
"God, I have sinned   against Thy holy name.
2370   Forgive the sins,   the great ones and the less,
That I committed   from my first hour of life
To this last day   when I have been struck down."
And now toward God   he raises his right glove;
A flight of angels   comes from the skies above. AOI

176

And now Count Roland,   lying beneath a pine,
Has turned his face   to look toward pagan Spain;
And he begins   remembering these things:

The many lands   his valor won the King,
Sweet France, his home,   the men of his own line,
And Charlemagne   who raised him in his house—   *2380*
The memories   make him shed tears and sigh.
But not forgetting   how close he is to death,
He prays that God   forgive him all his sins:
"O my true Father,   O Thou who never lied,
Thou who delivered   Lazarus from the grave,
Who rescued Daniel   out of the lions' den,
Keep now my soul   from every peril safe,
Forgive the sins   that I have done in life."
Roland's right glove   he offers now to God.   *[martyrdom – divine approval]*
Saint Gabriel comes   and takes it from his hand.   *2390*
His head sinks down   to rest upon his arm;
Hands clasped in prayer,   Roland has met his end.
God sends from heaven   the angel Cherubin,
Holy Saint Michael   who saves us from the sea,
And with these two   the angel Gabriel flies.
Count Roland's soul   they bring to Paradise.

177

Roland is dead;   his soul rests now with God.
The Emperor Charles   rides into Roncevaux;
On every road,   on every mountain path,
On every foot,   on every bit of land,   *2400*
They find a body   of Frank or Saracen.
King Charles cries out,   "Fair nephew, where are you?
Where's the Archbishop?   Where is Count Oliver?
Where is Count Gerin,   and Gerier his friend?
Oton—where is he,   and noble Berenger,
Ivoire and Ivon,   those two I held so dear?
Tell me what happened   to Gascon Engelier,
Where are Duke Samson,   the valiant Anseïs,
And Old Gérard,   the Count of Roussillon?
Where are the Peers,   the Twelve who stayed behind?"   *2410*

What good is asking   when no one can reply?
"God!" says the King,   "Now have I cause to grieve,
For where was I   when fighting here began!"
He pulls his beard   in anguish and in pain;
The lords of France   are weeping bitter tears,
And twenty thousand   faint in their grief and fall.
Duke Naimon feels   great sorrow for them all.

178

There is not one   among those noble lords
Who can refrain   from shedding tears of grief:
2420   It is their sons,   their brothers that they mourn,
Their nephews, friends;   they weep for their liege lords.
Many among them   fall fainting to the ground.
Only Duke Naimon   can see what must be done;
He is the first   to tell the Emperor:
"Look up ahead,   two leagues from where we stand,
See how the dust   is rising from the road—
There are the pagans,   and surely not a few.
Ride after them!   Let us avenge our grief!"
"O God," says Charles,   "they are already far—
2430   Grant me this grace,   let me do what is right,
For they have stolen   the flower of sweet France!"
The King commands   Oton and Geboïn,
Thibault of Reims,   and also Count Milon:
"Guard well this field,   the valleys and the heights,
Let all the dead   remain just as they are,
But keep them safe   from lions and wild beasts;
Let no one touch them,   no servant and no squire—
I say to you,   let no man touch these dead
Until God brings us   back to this field again."
2440   They answer him   with reverence and love:
"Right Emperor,   dear lord, as you command."
These four will keep   a thousand knights at hand. AOI

179

The Emperor Charles   has all his trumpets sound.
The mighty lord   rides onward with his host;
They find the tracks   made by the Saracens,
And all together   follow them in pursuit.
When the King sees   that evening will come soon,
In a green meadow   he gets down from his horse,
Kneels on the ground   and prays almighty God
To make the sun   stop moving through the sky,   *2450*
Delay the night,   and let the day remain.
And then an angel,   who often spoke with him,
Came in great haste   to give him this command:
"Charles, speed you on!   The light won't fail you now.
God knows that you have lost   the flower of France.
You'll have your vengeance   on the vile Saracen!"
Already Charles   has mounted once again. AOI

180

For Charlemagne   God worked a miracle:
The sun stops moving;   it stands still in the sky.
The pagans flee,   the Franks pursue them hard,   *2460*
At Val-Tenebre   they overtake their foes;
Toward Saragossa   they chase them, sword in hand,
With mighty blows   cutting the pagans down,
Driving them off   the wide paths and the roads,
Until they find   the Ebro in their way.
Deep is the water,   and frightening and swift,
There are no boats,   no galleys, not a barge.
The Saracens   invoke their Tervagant;
They all jump in,   but nothing keeps them safe.
The men in armor   weigh more than all the rest;   *2470*
Some of them sink   straight down into the depths,
Others are carried   by the swift-running stream.

Those lucky ones   still swallow just as much,
But with more time   to suffer as they go.
The Franks exult: "Roland brought you to woe!" AOI

181

When Charlemagne   sees all the pagans dead,
Some slain in battle,   and many of them drowned,
Leaving great spoils   for all the Frankish knights,
The noble King,   dismounting from his horse,
2480   Lies on the ground,   and gives his thanks to God.
When he gets up,   he sees the sun has set.
The Emperor says,   "We'll have to make camp here.
It's too late now   to ride to Roncevaux—
All of our horses   are weary and worn out.
Take off their saddles   and let their bridles go;
Free in these meadows,   they'll cool off as they should."
The Franks reply,   "My lord, your words are good." AOI

182

The Emperor Charles   has had his camp set up.
The French dismount   there in the wilderness,
2490   The horses' saddles   are taken off their backs,
The golden bridles   are lifted from their heads,
They roam the meadows   where there is good fresh grass—
There are no other   provisions to be had.
Men who are weary   lie on the ground and sleep;
For on this night   there is no watch to keep.

183

Now in a meadow   the Emperor lies down;
His mighty spear   he keeps close by his head,

For on this night   he wishes to stay armed.
He wears his hauberk   of saffron-burnished steel,
His helm is laced,   bright gems gleam in its gold;   *2500*
Still at his side,   Joyeuse, the peerless sword,
Which changes color   thirty times every day.
We all have heard   about the holy lance
With which Our Lord   was wounded on the Cross:
Charles has the spearhead—   almighty God be thanked—
He had it mounted   into the golden hilt,
And for that honor,   that sign of heaven's love,
The name Joyeuse   was given to the sword.
Let the French barons   remember this each time
They cry "Montjoie!"   in battle: let them know   *2510*
That war-cry means   they'll conquer any foe.

184

The night is clear,   the moon gleams in the sky.
King Charles lies down,   but for Count Roland grieves,
For Oliver   whose loss weighs on his heart,
For the Twelve Peers,   for all the men of France:
At Roncevaux   their bloodstained bodies lie.
He can't help weeping,   and bitterly laments,
Praying that God   have mercy on their souls.
The King is weary,   exhausted by his grief,
He falls asleep—   that's all that he can do.   *2520*
In all the meadows   the Franks are sleeping too.
There's not one horse   left standing on its feet;
Those who want grass   eat just what they can reach.
A man does well   to learn what pain can teach.

185

Charles goes to sleep   worn out by grief and toil.
Then God in heaven   sends Saint Gabriel down,

Commanding him   to guard the Emperor.
The angel stays   close by his head all night,
And in two visions   lets him see what will come:
2530   Another foe   is marching on the King,
The dream shows clearly   the fighting will be grim.
The Emperor sees   above him in the sky
Lightning and thunder,   and gusts of wind and hail;
Great are the tempests,   fearful and vast the storms.
The heavens gather   flickering fire and flames
Which all at once   fall down upon his men;
Ash-wood and apple,   their spear-shafts are ablaze,
Their shields are burning   down to the boss of gold,
The shafts snap off   from their keen-bladed spears,
2540   Their chain-mail crumples   and their strong helms of steel.
With great dismay   Charles sees his knights attacked
By vicious beasts—   by leopards and by bears,
Serpents and vipers,   dragons and devils too,
And there are griffons,   thirty thousand and more,
All of them leaping,   charging against the Franks,
The Franks who cry,   "Charlemagne, help us now!"
And overwhelmed   by pity and by grief,
He starts out toward them,   but something interferes:
A mighty lion   springs at him from a wood,
2550   Fearful to look at,   raging and proud and bold;
He leaps, attacking   the person of the King.
Grappling each other   they wrestle violently:
But who will rise   a victor, who will fall?
The Emperor sleeps   and does not wake at all.

186

Later that night   he had another dream:
He was in Aix   up on a block of stone;
There was a bear   bound tight with double chains.

2556. The word *perrun* means essentially a block of stone, whether it is a
mounting block, a place where the king sits on formal occasions, or one of the
stones on which Roland tries to break Durendal.

Thirty more bears   came out of the Ardennes,
Each of them speaking   exactly like a man.
They said to Charles,   "Sire, give him back to us!   *2560*
It isn't right   for you to keep him here;
We cannot choose   but bring our kinsman help."
Out of the palace   there came a hunting dog
Who then attacked   the largest of the bears;
On the green grass   apart from all the rest,
While the King watched,   they fought a dreadful fight—
He could not see   which one of them would lose.
All this God's angel   revealed to Charlemagne.
The King slept on   until it was bright day.

187

To Saragossa   the pagan King has fled.   *2570*
There he dismounts   beneath an olive tree,
Gives up his sword,   his hauberk and his helm;
On the green grass   the King lies down in shame.
Marsile's right hand   was cut completely off,
And he is fainting   from loss of blood and pain.
In front of him,   his wife Queen Bramimonde,
Weeping for grief,   cries out a loud lament.
The Queen has with her   some twenty thousand men,
All of them cursing   Charlemagne and sweet France.
Now they attack   Apollo in his crypt,   *2580*
Reviling him,   disfiguring his form:
"Why, evil god,   have you brought us to shame?
Why have you suffered   the downfall of our King?
For faithful service   you give a poor reward!"
Then they take off   his scepter and his crown,
And to a column   they tie him by the hands;
They knock him down,   stamping him with their feet,
And with great clubs   they smash him into bits.
They take the ruby   away from Tervagant,
And then Mohammed   they thrust into a ditch   *2590*
Where he'll be trampled   and gnawed by dogs and pigs.

188

When King Marsile   recovers from his faint,
They carry him   into his vaulted room
Where bright designs   are painted on the walls.
And Bramimonde,   the Queen, comes weeping there,
Tearing her hair,   deploring her sad fate;
In bitter grief   she cries these words aloud:
"O Saragossa,   how you have been despoiled!
You've lost that King   who was your noble lord!
2600   We are betrayed,   abandoned by our gods,
Those gods who failed him   this morning on the field.
The great Emir   will do a craven thing
Unless he comes   and fights these valiant Franks
Too proud to care   whether they live or die.
As for King Charles   whose flowing beard is white—
He has great valor;   he's arrogant and bold.
If there's a battle   he's sure to stand his ground.
Alas! that no one   can bring this hero down!"

189

The Emperor Charles   by force of arms has stayed
2610   Seven long years   at war in pagan Spain.
He's taken castles   and conquered many towns.
The King, Marsile,   has tried hard to resist.
In the first year   he sent a message, sealed,
To Baligant,   Emir of Babylon.
Ancient of days   was this most noble lord—
He had outlived   Virgil and Homer both:
Let him bring help   to Saragossa's King,
Or else Marsile   will cast away his gods,
Give up the idols   to which he always prayed,

2609. This is the beginning of the Baligant episode. It is also the second time
that the poet returns to the beginning of his poem, as in 703.

And turn instead   to holy Christian law,   *2620*
Ask Charlemagne   to set the terms for peace.
But Baligant,   far off, has long delayed;
From forty kingdoms   he had his vassals come.
Now great swift ships   prepare to cross the sea,
Galleys and barges   and sailing craft for war.
There is a harbor   near Alexandria
Where Baligant   makes ready all his fleet;
In early summer,   during the month of May
His pagan hosts   at last get under way.

190

Great is the might   of those vile infidels;   *2630*
They go by sail,   they use their oars and steer.
Up on the masts   and set in the high prows
Are many lanterns   and ruby-colored stones
Which from above   send forth such beams of light
That all night long   the sea is beautiful.
When they come close,   ready to land in Spain,
Their brightness passing   lights up the countryside,
And King Marsile   soon learns they have arrived. AOI

191

The pagan hosts,   impatient of delay,
Turn from the sea   and take the river road,   *2640*
Passing Marbrise,   leaving Marbrose behind,
Along the Ebro   speeds their enormous fleet.
The ships are sparkling   with lanterns and red stones
Which through the darkness   illuminate their way.
At Saragossa   they anchor the next day. AOI

2634. Jewels, particularly "carbuncles," were commonly considered sources of
illumination.

192

Fair is the morning,   the sun shines clear and bright.
Now from his ship   the Emir disembarks,
Espanaliz   comes forward on his right;
Seventeen kings   are following their lord,
2650   And I can't tell you   how many dukes and counts.
Under a laurel   which in a meadow stands,
A white silk carpet   is spread on the green grass;
An ivory throne   is set on it, and there
The Emir sits,   the pagan Baligant,
With all the others   remaining on their feet.
Their overlord   was the first one to speak:
"Listen to me,   you noble, valiant knights!
King Charlemagne,   Emperor of the Franks,
Has not the right to eat,   if I say no.
2660   He has waged war   through all my lands in Spain;
Now, in return,   I'll seek him in sweet France—
I won't give up,   while life is left in me,
Until he's dead,   or bows to his defeat."
Baligant strikes   his right glove on his knee.

193

Once he has said it,   nothing will change his mind—
All the world's gold   could not dissuade him now—
He'll go to Aix   where Charlemagne holds court;
Then all his vassals   praise him and so advise.
Baligant summons   two of his chevaliers,
2670   One, Clarifan,   the other Clarien:
"You are the sons   of King Maltraïen
Who served me often   as my ambassador.

2668. Some commentators have noted a contrast here between the autocratic
Baligant and Charlemagne's more democratic tendencies. It is certainly true that
Charlemagne asks for and accepts the advice of his council, providing they suggest nothing outrageous (262), and that the poet calls our attention to this most
emphatically (166–167).

It is my will   that you go to Marsile
In Saragossa;   tell him that I have come
To bring him help   against the men of France:
Given the chance,   I'll wage a mighty war.
Take with you, folded,   this gold-embroidered glove;
Let the King set   this pledge on his right hand,
And give Marsile   this envoy's staff of gold.
Say I expect   his homage for his fief.   *2680*
I'll go to France   and challenge Charlemagne,
And he will beg   for mercy at my feet.
He will renounce   his Christianity,
Or else I'll take   the crown right off his head!"
The pagans say,   "He'll be your man or dead."

194

Baligant says,   "You barons, mount and ride!
One take the staff,   the other take the glove."
And they reply,   "Dear lord, as you command."
They gallop on,   and come into the town;
There are ten gates,   four bridges that they cross,   *2690*
They pass through streets   where all the townsfolk live,
And as they climb   up to the highest place
They hear an uproar   inside the palace walls:
There are great numbers   of pagan Saracens
Weeping and shouting   and crying out in pain,
Mourning the gods,   Mohammed, Tervagant,
Apollo too,   which they possess no more.
They all are saying,   "What will become of us?
We are struck down   and utterly destroyed,
For we have lost   our rightful king, Marsile: *2700*
Just yesterday,   Roland cut off his hand;
Nor shall we see   blond Jurfaleu again.
Now all of Spain   surrenders to that Count!"
The messengers   from Baligant dismount.

2691. Burgeis—the oldest known occurrence of this word (Jenkins).

195

They leave their horses   beneath an olive tree;
Two Saracens   have taken up the reins.
The envoys, holding   each other by the cloak,
Enter the palace,   go up long flights of stairs,
And when they reach   the King's high-vaulted room,
2710   Their courtesy   offers ill-chosen words:
"We pray Mohammed,   who has us in his care,
Our lord Apollo   and mighty Tervagant,
To save the King   and to protect the Queen!"
Bramimonde says,   "Who speaks that way is mad!
Those gods of ours   are traitors one and all.
At Roncevaux   they worked such miracles
That our brave knights   were slaughtered by the Franks;
As for my husband,   they failed him in the fight,
And his right hand   was cut completely off—
2720   That mighty lord   Count Roland did the deed.
This land of Spain   will all belong to Charles!
Wretched, abandoned,   what is my destiny?
If you were kind,   you'd make an end to me!" AOI

196

Says Clarien,   "Lady, don't talk so much!
We are the envoys   of pagan Baligant.
He guarantees   protection for Marsile—
In pledge of that   he sends this staff and glove.
Out on the Ebro   we have four thousand boats,
Sailing ships, barges,   swift-running galleys too,
2730   And other vessels,   more than a man could count.
The great Emir   is powerful and rich;
He will go hunting   for Charlemagne in France,
And make him choose: the pagan faith or death."
Bramimonde says,   "No need to go so far!
It's where you are right now   you'll find the Franks!

For seven years   they've overrun this land.
A fighting lord   is Charles their Emperor—
He'd rather die   than run from any field;
No king on earth   but seems to him a child.
Charles has no fear   of any man alive!"   *2740*

197

"Now that's enough!"   Marsile says to the Queen,
And to the envoys: "Address yourselves to me.
My lords, you see   that I am close to death;
I have no son,   no daughter, and no heir—
The one I had   was killed just yesterday.
Say to my lord   that I would see him here.
The Emir Baligant   has rights in Spain;
He'll have my kingdom,   if that is his desire—
But let him guard it well   against the Franks!
I'll give him counsel   regarding Charlemagne: *2750*
He'll hold him captive   just one month from today.
Here are the keys   to Saragossa's walls;
Tell the Emir   to trust me and remain."
"My lord," they answer,   "your words are true and plain." AOI

198

Marsile says this: "The Emperor of France
Killed all my men,   my kingdom he laid waste,
My towns and cities   he captured and destroyed.
He lay last night   close to the Ebro's banks;
I know the distance—   not more than seven leagues.
Tell the Emir   to lead his army there.   *2760*
Give him my message: the time is ripe for war."
Keys of the city   he sends to Baligant;
Both messengers   bow low to King Marsile
And go their way   when they have taken leave.

199

Now the two envoys   have mounted once again;
They leave the city   as fast as they can go.
With great excitement   they rush to their Emir,
Give him the keys   to Saragossa's walls.
Baligant says,   "And what have you found out?
2770   Where is Marsile   whom I had summoned here?"
Clarien says,   "He's wounded unto death.
King Charles was crossing   the mountains yesterday,
For he intended   to go back to sweet France;
His noblest barons   were left to guard the pass:
The King's own nephew,   Count Roland, stayed behind,
Oliver too—   all the Twelve Peers of France,
And twenty thousand   were with them, valiant knights.
They were attacked   by the brave King Marsile;
When he and Roland   met on the battlefield,
2780   Durendal struck him   so terrible a blow
That his right hand   was severed from his arm;
His son was killed,   whom he so dearly loved,
And all the barons   who fought there at his side.
He fled the battle—   he could not stand his ground—
And Charlemagne   pursued him off the field.
King Marsile swears   that if you save him now
You'll take possession   of all the lands of Spain."
And Baligant   listens to news so bad
With thoughts so painful   they nearly drive him mad. AOI

200

2790   "My lord Emir,"   continues Clarien,
"Just yesterday   they fought at Roncevaux.
Roland was killed,   and so was Oliver,

2772. "Yesterday" should perhaps not be taken literally. Similarly, line 2791.

All the Twelve Peers   whom Charlemagne held dear,
And twenty thousand,   the warriors of France.
There King Marsile   had his right hand cut off,
The Emperor Charles   pursued him off the field;
In all this kingdom   no chevalier is left—
They all were slain,   or in the Ebro drowned.
Close to the river   the French have made their camp:
From where we stand,   the distance is so short   *2800*
That, if you wish it,   they'll have a hard road home."
Now Baligant   looks fierce and proud again;
Great is the joy   he feels within his heart.
All of a sudden   he leaps up to his feet
Shouting aloud,   "My barons, get you gone!
Out of the boats!   Now is the time to ride!
If we don't let   old Charlemagne escape,
For King Marsile   prompt payment I'll demand,
And send him back a head   for his right hand."

201

The Arab pagans,   leaving their boats behind,   *2810*
With all speed mount   their horses and their mules,
And ride away—   that's what they're told to do.
The great Emir   who roused their will to war
Summons Gemalfin,   a man that he held dear:
"While I am gone,   my hosts are in your care."
He mounts a dark brown war-horse,   and rides away;
Four noble dukes   follow him close behind.
At Saragossa   he rides into the town,
And then draws rein   beside a marble block;
Four counts are there   to hold the stirrups taut   *2820*
While he dismounts.   He climbs the palace stairs,
And Bramimonde   comes running up to him,
Crying aloud,   "Alas that I was born!
I've lost my husband;   Sire, I am left to shame."

He lifts her up,   as she falls at his feet;
Now they have gone   to King Marsile's retreat.

202

When King Marsile   sees Baligant come in,
He quickly summons   two Spanish Saracens:
"Give me your help—   I want to sit up straight."
2830   In his left hand   he holds one of his gloves.
Then says Marsile,   "My lord and King, Emir,
All of these lands . . .
And Saragossa   with all it holds in fief.
I've brought myself to ruin,   my people too."
The Emir answers,   "I grieve to learn of this,
And there's no time for us   to talk at length—
Charles isn't waiting,   I know, to fight with me,
But just the same   I do accept your glove."
And so, in sorrow,   weeping, he turns away. AOI
2840   He leaves the palace,   down the long flights of stairs,
Gets on his horse   and spurs back to his men.
He gallops hard   until he leads them all;
Often he shouts   to urge them to the fray,
"Pagans, come on!   Don't let them get away!" AOI

203

Early next morning   when the bright dawn appears,
The Emperor Charles   awakens from his sleep.
Saint Gabriel,   whom God sent to keep watch,
Blesses the King,   making his holy sign.
Charlemagne rises;   he takes his armor off.
2850   Throughout the hosts,   men put their weapons down;
They mount their horses,   and ride with utmost speed
Down the long paths,   along the broad straight road.

They will have cause   for wonder and great woe,
There where the battle   was fought at Roncevaux. AOI

204

King Charlemagne   returns to Roncevaux.
He sees the dead;   his eyes are filled with tears.
He tells the Franks,   "My lords, walk slowly on;
I'll go before you   into the battlefield—
I know I'll find   my nephew's body there.
One time at Aix   during a solemn feast,   2860
My valiant knights   were making boastful vows
To fight great battles   and do heroic deeds.
I heard my nephew   say he could promise this:
If he must die   fighting in some strange land,
We'd find his body   beyond his men and peers,
His head still turned   to face the enemy;
He'd end his life   in valor, conquering."
A greater distance   than flies a stick well thrown,
He goes ahead,   then climbs a hill alone.

205

The Emperor, seeking   the place where Roland fell,   2870
Crosses a meadow   covered with plants whose flowers
Are all stained crimson   with the life-blood of France.
He feels such sorrow   he cannot help but weep.
And now he finds,   close to the two great trees,
Three blocks of stone   where Durendal cut deep;
On the green grass   he sees his nephew, dead.
It is no wonder   he's overwhelmed with woe.
The King dismounts   and runs across the field.
He takes Count Roland   and holds him in his arms,
Falls with him, fainting,   his grief so racks his heart.   2880

206

The Emperor Charles   recovers from his faint;
Naimon the Duke,   with him Count Acelin,
Geoffroy of Anjou,   his brother called Thierry,
Go to the King,   raise him beneath a pine.
And Charles looks down;   he sees his nephew dead.
With words of praise,   softly, he says farewell:
"Roland, my friend,   may God forgive your sins!
Never on earth   was there a knight like you
To fight great battles   in triumph to the end.
2890   From this time forth   my honor will decline."
He cannot help it: he faints a second time. AOI

207

The Emperor   recovers consciousness;
Four of his barons   support him by his hands;
King Charles looks down   at Roland lying dead,
So handsome still,   but he is ashen pale,
His eyes turned upward,   dark shadows in their place.
Then Charlemagne   with love and faith laments:
"Roland, my friend,   may your soul rest in flowers
In Paradise,   among the holy saints!
2900   The fault is mine   that you found death in Spain!
No day will dawn   but that I'll grieve for you.
This is the end   of all my strength and pride!
Who will uphold   Charlemagne's honor now?
In all the world   there's no friend left to me;

2900. *Cum en Espaigne venis a mal seignur!*, important for the interpretation
of the poem, is unfortunately open to various meanings. If one reads *seignur* as
a vocative, Charles would express regret for Roland's death and possibly for his
having come to Spain at all. Otherwise, it would be an expression of self-
reproach on the Emperor's part. Bédier and Segre, both with some hesitation,
and Jenkins emphatically, prefer this reading.

I have no kinsmen   so worthy and so brave."
With both his hands   he tears his silver hair.
The sight so moves   a hundred thousand Franks
There is not one   dry-eyed in all their ranks. AOI

208

"Roland, my friend,   I'm going home to France;
There in Laon   when I hold court once more,   *2910*
Strangers will come   from kingdoms all around,
And they will ask me,   'Where is the chieftain Count?'
And I will tell them   that Roland died in Spain.
In bitter sorrow   my kingdom I will keep;
No day will dawn   when I don't mourn and weep."

209

"Roland, my friend,   valiant and young and fair,
Aix la Chapelle   will see my court again,
And men will come   asking to hear the news.
I'll give them tidings   cruel and full of woe:
'Dead is my nephew   who won me such great lands.'   *2920*
Against my rule   the Saxons will rebel,
Hungarians, Bulgars,   so many pagan tribes,
Romans, Apulians,   the men of Sicily,
And Africans,   and men of Califerne;
A time of toil   and hardship will begin—
Who will command   my hosts to victory,
Since he is dead   who led us in the field?
Alas, sweet France!   How empty you will be!
I feel such sorrow   I wish I were no more."
King Charlemagne   pulls at his silver beard;   *2930*
He tears his hair,   twisting it with both hands.
A hundred thousand   fall fainting where they stand.

210

"Roland, my friend,   alas for your young life!
Now may your soul   rejoice in Paradise!
Whoever killed you   struck down the pride of France.
I feel such sorrow   I have no wish to live,
Mourning those men   who died here serving me.
I pray that God,   the blessed Mary's son,
Will let me die   before I come to Cize,
2940   That soul and body   part company today.
Among their souls   mine too would have its place,
My flesh and theirs   be buried side by side."
He pulls his beard   and from his eyes tears flow.
Duke Naimon says,   "Now Charles feel bitter woe." AOI

211

"Lord Emperor,"   Geoffroy of Anjou says,
"Control yourself;   do not give way to grief.
Have the field searched   for bodies of our men
Killed in the battle   by Spanish Saracens,
And to one grave   command that they be borne."
2950   The King replies,   "So be it; sound your horn!" AOI

212

Geoffroy of Anjou   has blown a trumpet call;
The French dismount   at Charlemagne's command
To seek their friends,   dead on the battlefield,
And put their bodies   into a common grave.
The many bishops   and abbots who are there,

2935. Perhaps the poet meant to remind his audience that Roland died not of battle wounds but of the injury he suffered in the tremendous effort of blowing the Oliphant.

The monks and canons   and all the tonsured priests
Absolve the dead   and sign them with the cross.
They kindle incense,   light aromatic myrrh:
From swinging censers   arise sweet clouds of smoke.
They closed the grave   with all the rites they knew,   *2960*
And turned away—   what else was there to do? AOI

213

Then Charles has Roland   made ready for the grave,
And Oliver,   Archbishop Turpin too,
Their chests cut open   while he himself looks on,
The three men's hearts   withdrawn and wrapped in silk,
And in a coffin   of pure white marble placed.
When that is done,   the bodies of the lords
Are taken up   and washed with spice and wine;
Around each baron   they place a deerskin shroud.
Charlemagne orders   Thibault and Geboin,   *2970*
Milon the Count   and the Marquis Oton
To lead the carts   in which they were conveyed,
All covered over   with palls of silk brocade. AOI

214

The Emperor Charles   is anxious to depart,
But pagan outposts   rise up along his way.
Then from the closest,   two messengers arrive;
For Baligant,   they summon Charles to war:
"This is no time,   proud King, to go away!
The great Emir   is riding on your heels
With all the hosts   he led across the sea.   *2980*
We'll know today   what courage you command!" AOI
At that King Charles,   his hand upon his beard,
Thinks once again   of all that he has lost.
With fiery pride   he gazes at his men,

Then in a voice   mighty and clear he cries,
"Barons of France,   take up your arms and ride!" AOI

215

King Charles is first   to arm himself for war.
Wasting no time,   he puts his hauberk on,
Laces his helm;   Joyeuse hangs at his side,
2990   The blade whose brilliance   outshines the very sun.
Around his neck   the King has placed his shield;
He brandishes   the steel point of his spear;
And now he mounts   his good horse Tencendur,
Won in a battle   close to Marsone's ford
Where Charles' spear felled   Malpalin of Narbonne.
He frees the reins,   and spurring quick and hard,
Before the host   he gallops on parade; AOI
God and Saint Peter   he summons to his aid.

216

All through the field   the men of France dismount;
3000   A hundred thousand   put on their gear for war.
They have equipment   such as their hearts desire,
Beautiful weapons   and horses bred for speed.
Mounted, they look   as if they'd fight with skill;
Given a chance,   they'll prove it on the field.
Their battle-flags   hang down to touch their helms.
Charlemagne sees   their gallant war-like mien,
And says these words   to Jozeran of Provence,
Naimon the Duke,   Antelme of Mayence:
"In such brave knights   a man can place his trust;
3010   Only a fool,   with such a host, despairs.
And if these Arabs   don't change their minds and flee,
The price they'll pay   for Roland won't be low."
Duke Naimon answers, "God grant that it be so." AOI

217

Charlemagne summons   Rabel and Guinemant,
And says to them,   "My lords, hear my command:
In Roland's place   and Oliver's you'll ride;
One bear the sword,   and one the Oliphant.
You two shall be   the leaders of my host,
And you'll be followed   by fifteen thousand Franks,
Young nobles all,   the bravest in the land.   *3020*
And after these,   as many men again
Will be commanded   by Geboin and Lodrant."
Naimon the Duke,   with him Count Jozeran,
Set these divisions   in order for the field.
If there's a battle,   they won't be quick to yield. AOI

218

The first divisions   are filled up by the French,
And after these   they organize a third.
The vassals in it   are all Bavarians,
Their forces number   some twenty thousand knights.
These men in battle   will never break their line;   *3030*
In all the world   King Charles holds none so dear
Except the French   who won him all his realm.
Because their fierceness   has won these warriors fame,
A great man will lead them: Ogier the Dane. AOI

219

The Emperor Charles   has three divisions now;
Naimon the Duke   establishes a fourth
Made up of barons,   loyal and very brave,
The Alemans   who come from Germany.
The others count them   as twenty thousand men.
They're well equipped   with horses and with arms;   *3040*

Not even death   can make them quit the field.
These soldiers Herman,   the Duke of Thrace, will lead;
He'd rather die   than do a coward's deed. AOI

220

And then Duke Naimon,   with him Count Jozeran,
Formed a division   of men from Normandy,
Some twenty thousand,   according to the Franks.
They have fine weapons,   swift-running horses too;
Not even death   will ever make them yield.
No better fighters   exist in all the world;
3050   Richard the Old   will lead them in the fray—
Many a pagan   his sharpened spear will slay. AOI

221

The sixth division,   made up of Breton knights,
Has thirty thousand   among its chevaliers,
A noble sight   as they ride forth to war
Their lances straight,   with waving battle-flags.
A man called Eudon   is leader of these men.
This is the order   he gives Count Nevelon,
Thibault of Reims,   and the Marquis Oton:
"You'll take the lead;   this honor you have won."

222

3060   The Emperor Charles   has six divisions now;
Duke Naimon starts   to make a seventh one:
Men of Poitou,   and lords of the Auvergne.
Some forty thousand   number these chevaliers,
All with good horses   and the best kind of arms.

These, in a valley   protected by a hill,
Are grouped apart;   Charles blessed them with his hand.
Godselme and Jozeran   are in command.

223

The eighth division   Duke Naimon organized,
Made up of Flemings   and knights from Friedland too,
Has forty thousand   among its ranks, and more.   3070
These are not likely   to run away from war.
Thus spoke the King: "They'll serve me very well."
Hamon of Galicia   and Rembalt too
Will lead these troops,   and knightly deeds they'll do.

224

After that, Naimon,   with him Count Jozeran,
Made up another   brigade of valiant men,
Some from Lorraine,   others from Burgundy;
They say it numbered   some fifty thousand knights.
Their helms are laced,   they have their hauberks on,
Their spears are heavy   with shafts cut very short.   3080
If any Arabs   venture to come their way,
They'll strike them down   until the war is won;
They follow Thierry,   the Duke of the Argonne. AOI

225

The tenth division   has none but lords of France,
The best of chieftains,   a hundred thousand strong.
Powerful looking,   their bearing fierce and proud;
Their heads and beards   are glistening with white.
They wear mail hauberks   and byrnies double thick;

They gird on swords   which come from France or Spain,
3090   Their shields are bright   with colors and designs.
And now they mount,   all asking for the fight,
"Montjoie!" they cry;   with them rides Charlemagne.
Geoffroy of Anjou   carries the Oriflamme—
It was Saint Peter's,   and then was called Romaine;
Among the Franks   Montjoie has been its name.

226

The Emperor stops,   dismounting from his horse,
To lie prostrate,   face down on the green grass.
He looks eastward   into the rising sun.
He calls on God,   and prays most earnestly:
3100   "Father in Heaven,   protect me on this day
As Thou in truth   didst rescue Jonah once
When he was captured   and held inside a whale,
As Thou didst spare   the King of Nineveh,
And rescued Daniel   from fearful suffering
When he was thrown   inside the lion's den;
And those three children   set in the midst of flames—
So may Thy love   be close to me today!
And in Thy mercy   be gracious to my plea
That Roland's vengeance   may be allowed to me."
3110   His prayer finished,   King Charles stands up again;
Crossing himself,   in token of God's power.
And then the King   mounts his swift-running horse,
His stirrup held   by Naimon, Jozeran;
He takes his shield   and his sharp-pointed spear.
A handsome man,   the Emperor, and strong,
His face is calm,   his bearing very proud;

3090. Identifying insignia.
3094. Charlemagne's banner.
3110. Noting a capital letter beginning this line, Segre starts a new *laisse* here, but the assonance is uninterrupted.

He rides to battle,   as one with his great horse.
The clear-voiced trumpets   ring out from every side—
Above the others   resounds Count Roland's horn;
Then all the Frenchmen   remember him and mourn.   *3120*

227

In all his splendor   the Emperor rides on.
Outside his hauberk   he shows his long white beard;
For love of him,   the others do the same:
So were distinguished   his hundred thousand Franks.
They cross those mountains   crested with rocky peaks,
Those deep-set valleys,   those dark and narrow ways,
Out of the pass,   through the wastelands again—
Once more for Spain   the Franks have set their course.
On a plateau   they make camp for the night.
The pagan outposts   return to Baligant,   *3130*
And now a Syrian   tells what they have to say:
"Our eyes have seen   the arrogant King Charles.
His men are proud;   nothing will make them flee.
Take up your arms!   The battle is at hand!"
Says Baligant,   "Brave news, and I rejoice.
Summon my pagans   by the shrill trumpet's voice!"

228

Throughout the host   now beat the pagan drums,
Clarion horns   and clear-voiced trumpets sound.
The men dismount   to arm themselves for war.
The great Emir,   impatient of delay,   *3140*
Puts on a byrnie   of saffron-burnished mail,
Laces his helmet   shining with gold and jewels.
At his left side,   Baligant girds his sword
Which in his pride   he honored with a name:
He had been told   of Charlemagne's Joyeuse,

And so he called   his own sword Précieuse;
He chose that name   to be his war-cry too.
He has it shouted   by all his chevaliers.
Around his neck   he places his broad shield,
3150   Its boss is gold   with crystal all around,
The strap embroidered   with circles on brocade;
The spear he holds   has Evil for its name,
Its mighty shaft   looks like a rafter beam;
The tip itself   would overload a mule.
Now Baligant   has mounted his great horse,
The stirrup held   by Marcules d'Oltremer.
To carry him   a horse needs a broad back;
The Emir's hips are slender,   his chest is wide
With well-sprung ribs,   and beautifully shaped;
3160   He has broad shoulders,   a brightness in his face,
A proud expression;   his head of curling hair
Is just as white   as any summer flower.
As for his courage,   he's proved it many times.
God! What a hero,   if he had been baptized!
He spurs his horse—   the bright red blood spurts out—
And gallops forward,   leaping a mighty ditch:
Some fifty feet   it measures at the least.
The pagans cry,   "This lord will lose no lands!
If any Frenchman   should dare to joust with him,
3170   He'll have no choice   but swiftly will be slain;
Charles is a fool   for choosing to remain!" AOI

229

This Baligant   looks like a noble lord.
His shining beard   is white as any flower.
He has great wisdom   concerning pagan law,
And once in battle   he's arrogant and fierce.
He has a son,   Malpramis, a fine knight,

3152. "Maltet."

Powerful, tall,   resembling his forebears.
"Sire, let's ride on!"   he says to Baligant,
"I'll be surprised   if we find Charlemagne."
His father answers,   "He's valiant; he'll be there.   3180
The chronicles   give him the highest praise.
But since Count Roland,   his nephew, is no more,
He has no power   to challenge us in war." AOI

230

"Fair son, Malpramis,"   the Emir said to him,
"Just yesterday,   that noble knight was slain,
Oliver too,   so valiant and so wise,
All the Twelve Peers   King Charles once held so dear,
And twenty thousand   who came with them from France.
All of the others   I count not worth a glove.
The Emperor Charles   is coming back again;   3190
My messenger,   the Syrian, reports
That ten divisions   are under his command.
A valiant lord   now sounds the Oliphant,
From his companion   a trumpet call comes back:
These two are riding   as leaders of the host,
And they are followed   by fifteen thousand Franks
Charles calls his children: brave warriors, and young.
The next division   is just as large again.
These men will fight   with all the pride they show."
Malpramis says,   "Then let me have first blow." AOI   3200

231

"Fair son, Malpramis,"   says Baligant to him,
"You shall be granted   the boon that you have asked;

3189. The modern reader is sensitive to the importance of gloves in this poem,
but Baligant uses the figurative meaning: something without value.

Against the Franks,   and soon, you'll strike your blow.
You shall have with you   Torleu, the Persian King,
And Dapamort,   the ruler of the Wilzes.
If you succeed   in putting down French pride,
You'll call your own   that portion of my land
From Cheriant   as far as Val-Marchis."
Malpramis answers,   "My lord, you have my thanks."
3210   Then coming forward,   the Prince receives that gift,
The realm that once   belonged to King Florit;
The land is given   in such an evil hour
He'll never see it,   or hold it in his power.

232

The great Emir   goes riding through his hosts,
With tall Malpramis   following close behind.
Then the two Kings,   Torleu and Dapamort,
Thirty divisions   establish with all speed;
Great is the number   of knights assembled there,
With fifty thousand   forming the least brigade.
3220   The first division   has men of Butentrot,
And in the second   big-headed men from Misnes—
They have stiff hairs   growing along their spines
Just like the bristles   along the backs of pigs. AOI
The third is formed   of Nubles men and Blos,
The fourth division   contains the Bruns and Slavs,
And in the fifth   they place Sorbres and Sors;
Then in the sixth   Armenians and Moors,
And in the seventh   the men from Jerico;
The eighth are blacks,   the ninth composed of Gros,
3230   The tenth all come   from Balide la Forte—
There is a tribe   which never loved the good! AOI
Baligant vows   by what he holds most high,
Mohammed's body   and holy miracles:
"Now like a madman   comes riding Charles of France.

There'll be a battle,   unless he flees instead.
He'll wear no longer   a gold crown on his head!"

233

Ten more divisions   are made up after these:
The first contains   the ugly Canaanites
Who from Val-Foït   have made their way across;
The second, Turks;   Persians are in the third;   *3240*
The fourth contains   the savage Pinceneis,
The fifth has men   from Soltras and Avars;
The sixth has men   from Ormaleus, Eugiez,
And in the seventh   are Samuel's Bulgars;
The eighth from Bruise,   the ninth comes from Clavers,
The tenth from Occian   which on the desert lies—
There is a tribe   which never served our God—
You'll never hear   of any men more vile;
And they have hides   that are as hard as iron,
So they care nothing   for hauberk or for helm.   *3250*
There are no soldiers   more savage in the realm. AOI

234

Ten more divisions   the Emir formed himself:
The first made up   of giants from Malprose,
The second, Huns;   the third, Hungarians;
The fourth has men   from Baldise la Longue;
The fifth has men   who come from Val-Peneuse;
The sixth comes both   from . . . and Marose;
The seventh: Leus   and from Astrymonis,
The eighth from Argoille,   the ninth comes from Clarbonne,
The tenth division: long-bearded men from Fronde—   *3260*
There is a tribe   which has no love for God.
Thirty divisions   *Gesta Francorum* counts.

Great are the hosts   where those shrill trumpets play.
The pagans ride   like heroes to the fray. AOI

235

A mighty lord,   the Emir Baligant:
In front of him   his dragon-standard goes,
And then a banner,   the emblem of his gods;
There is an image   of vile Apollo too.
Ten Canaanites   on horseback ride around
3270 Shouting aloud   this sermon as they go:
"All those who hope   our gods will save them now,
Let them give heed: do penitence and pray!"
At that the pagans,   bowing their heads and chins,
Bring their bright helmets   down to the very ground.
The Frenchmen say,   "Soon, felons, you shall die!
May utter ruin   await you here today!
Heavenly Father,   protect King Charlemagne,
And let this battle   be given in his name!"

236

The great Emir,   experienced and wise,
3280 Calls to his presence   his son and the two Kings:
"My noble lords,   your place is at the head
Of my divisions;   you shall command them all,
Except for three   that I'll keep in reserve:
One will be Turkish,   another Ormaleis,
And for the third,   the giants of Malprose.
The men of Occiant   shall fight here at my side:
Those are the ones   who'll meet Charles and the French.
If Charlemagne   consents to fight with me,
There where his head is,   you'll see an empty space—
3290 Thus will his rights   be honored by my grace!" AOI

3278. The pronoun may refer to God.

237

Great are the hosts,   well ordered in brigades.
They see between them   no valley, hill or height,
No wood or forest   where ambush could be made:
They face each other   across a level plain.
Baligant says,   "My pagans, now's the time!
Mount up and ride—   our foes are on the field!
Amborre of Oluferne   shall bear my flag!"
Then all the pagans   are shouting, "Précieuse!"
The Frenchmen answer,   "May this day be your last!"
And once again   their cry rings out: "Montjoie!"   *3300*
The Emperor Charles   has his clear trumpets sound,
And Roland's horn   which heartens all the Franks.
The pagans say,   "Charles has good men with him.
We'll have a battle   most terrible and grim."

238

Wide is the field,   horizons far away.
The golden helmets,   set with fair jewels, gleam,
The ranks of shields,   the saffron-burnished mail,
And all the spears   with their bright flags of war.
The trumpets sound,   their voices clear and high;
The Oliphant   rings out above them all.   *3310*
Baligant summons   his brother to his side:
That's Canabeus,   the King of Floredée,
Who rules the land   as far as Val Sevrée.
The Emir points   at Charlemagne's brigade:
"Look at the pride   of celebrated France!
With what fierce courage   the Emperor sits his horse;
He's in the rear   among those veterans

3302. Thus the Oliphant was not, after all, destroyed.
3305. Turoldus emphasizes the difference between this battlefield and Roncevaux. Here, Good faces Evil out in the open.

Who wear their hauberks   with their long beards outside,
White as the snow   when it lies over ice.
3320 They'll strike keen blows   with lances and with swords—
Stubborn and fierce   will be our battle here,
Greater than any   seen in the world before."
You couldn't throw   a well-peeled stick as far
As he rides on,   ahead of all his men.
Then with these words,   he urges them to fight:
"Pagans, come on!   Follow! I'll lead the way!"
He shakes his spear,   to make his meaning plain,
And holds it high,   the point toward Charlemagne. AOI

239

The Emperor Charles   looks at the great Emir,
3330 His dragon-standard,   his banner and his flag,
The Arab forces   with their enormous hosts—
They've spread out over   the country on all sides,
Save for the land   he occupies himself.
Then Charlemagne   shouts in a mighty voice,
"Barons of France,   good vassals one and all!
You've fought and triumphed   in many hard campaigns!
Look at these pagans;   cowards they are, and vile!
The gods they worship   are not worth half a cent.
What does it matter   how many they may be?
3340 Let those men leave   who won't ride with me now!"
He digs his spurs   into his horse's side,
And Tencendur   leaps in the air four times.
"This is a valiant King,"   the Frenchmen say.
"Ride on, my lord,   we're with you, come what may !"

240

Fair was the day,   the sun shone bright and clear.
The splendid hosts   with their large companies

Move toward each other;   the first are face to face.
Count Guinemant,   and with him Count Rabel,
Let go their reins,   send their swift horses on,
Spurring them hard.   The warriors of France   *3350*
Gallop to strike   with pointed spear and lance. AOI

241

A valiant knight,   and strong, is Count Rabel.
He pricks his horse   with spurs of shining gold,
Charges and strikes   Torleu, the Persian King.
Hauberk and shield   cannot withstand that blow:
Rabel's gold spear   goes through him like a spit;
The King falls dead   on top of a small bush.
The Frenchmen say,   "Help us, almighty God!
Charles' cause is just;   we must not fail him now." AOI

242

Guinemant charges   a King of Leutice.   *3360*
His first blow shatters   the ornamented shield,
Then the King's hauberk   goes flying into bits;
Up to the standard   the spear has pierced his flesh;
Like it or not,   the pagan King falls dead.
Seeing that blow,   the men of France all shout,
"Now's the time, barons!   Go to it, strike them down!
Against these pagans,   the right is on Charles' side;
God sent us here   to have this good cause tried!" AOI

243

The Prince, Malpramis,   riding a pure white horse,
Forces his way   right through the throng of Franks,   *3370*

Meeting each one   with such prodigious blows
The dead pile up   behind him as he goes.
And then rings out   the voice of Baligant:
"Hear me, my barons,   I've nurtured you so long!
Look at my son,   he's hunting Charlemagne;
He wields his weapons   to challenge the French lords—
No better vassal   could any man desire.
Take up your spears!   Go out and help him now!"
Hearing these words,   the pagans charge the field;
3380   They strike hard blows   with all their might and main.
So wondrous fierce   the fighting grew, no war
Was ever like it,   since that time or before. AOI

244

Great are the hosts,   and proud their companies.
Now all divisions   are fighting on the field.
The pagan forces   strike with tremendous blows.
God! The spear shafts   splintered and cut in two,
The broken helmets,   the chain-mail split apart!
Pieces were strewn   like rushes on the ground.
The soft green grass   which covered all the field
3390   Was stained bright crimson   with French and pagan blood.
The Emir speaks   to urge his household on:
"Strike hard, my lords;   let's cut these Christians down!"
No men have fought   so stubbornly and hard
Ever before,   or since, on any field;
Until the nightfall,   nothing will make them yield. AOI

245

The great Emir   calls out to all his men:
"Strike them down, pagans,   that's what you came here for!
I'll give you wives,   well-born and beautiful,
I'll give you fiefdoms,   wide lands and fair domains."

The pagans answer,   "We'll do our part for that!"   *3400*
Their mighty blows   have cost them all their spears;
They draw their swords,   a hundred thousand strong.
Then there's a slaughter,   a cruel, grim melee;
They see a battle,   those men who dare to stay! AOI

246

The Emperor Charles   then calls upon his Franks:
"I've faith in you, my lords;   I hold you dear
For all the battles   you've fought and won for me,
The kingdoms conquered,   the kings you've helped depose—
I don't forget   what recompense is due
From my own body,   and gifts of land and gold.   *3410*
Avenge your sons,   your brothers and your heirs—
Just yesterday   they died at Roncevaux!
Against the pagans   you know I'm in the right."
The French reply,   "My lord, you speak the truth."
The twenty thousand   that Charles has close to him
As with one voice   proclaim their loyalty:
They will not fail him   for suffering or death.
Each one of them   strikes with a spear or lance,
And after that   they fight on, sword in hand.
Grim war they wage   at Charlemagne's command. AOI   *3420*

247

Prince Malpramis   rides through the battlefield,
And as he goes   he kills good men of France.
Naimon the Duke   watches with fiery eyes,
And then he charges,   the valiant chevalier;
His spear-point, passing   right through the upper shield,
Splits the gold border   where the chain-mail is joined.
Into the body   the yellow banner flies;
Malpramis falls   where seven hundred lie.

248

King Canabeus,   brother to the Emir,
3430 Urging his horse   with sharp pricks of the spur,
Unsheathes his sword   which has a crystal hilt.
He charges Naimon,   and strikes his princely helm;
One side of it   is shattered by the blow;
Five of the lacings   the steel blade slices through.
No one would give   two cents for that mail hood
Split by the sword   which reaches to the flesh—
Part of his scalp   is hurled down to the ground.
The Duke is stunned   by that tremendous blow;
He would have fallen,   but for the help of God.
3440 He puts his arms   around his horse's neck,
And if that pagan   had charged him just once more,
The noble lord   would certainly have died.
But Charles of France   comes riding to his side. AOI

249

Naimon the Duke   is in great need of help,
And Canabeus   hastens to strike again.
Charles says, "Vile serf,   you fought him to your woe!"
With mighty valor   he charges in and strikes;
He breaks the shield   against the pagan's heart,
The hauberk's neckpiece   yields to that fierce attack;
3450 An empty saddle   sits on the horse's back.

250

King Charlemagne   is overwhelmed with grief
When he sees Naimon   wounded before his eyes;
On the green grass   fall bright red drops of blood.
Then leaning toward him,   the Emperor says this:
"Naimon, fair lord,   come ride beside me now!
That wretched serf   who threatened you is dead:

I took my spear   and ran him through and through."
The Duke replies,   "My lord, I trust in you;
And if I live,   this debt shall be repaid."
In loyal friendship   they fight on side by side,   3460
With them the Franks,   some twenty thousand men,
Wield sword or spear   against the Saracens. AOI

251

The great Emir   goes riding through the field;
He turns to charge,   attacking Guinemant,
Whose shining shield   is crushed against his heart.
The hauberk cracks,   its panels split apart;
The spearhead crashes   right through the Frenchman's chest;
The Count is hurled   from his swift-running horse.
Then the Emir   killed Geboin and Lorant,
Richard the Old,   the lord of Normandy,   3470
The pagans say,   "That is a valiant blade.
With Précieuse   we cannot be afraid!" AOI

252

You should have seen   the knights of Araby,
Warriors of Occiant,   Bascle and Argoille!
Fiercely they strike,   wielding their spears and swords,
And yet the French   have no thought of retreat.
Not a few men   on both sides fall and die.
The battle rages   until the sky grows dark,
Great are the losses   among the Frankish lords;
They'll see more grief   before they end the war. AOI   3480

253

Both French and Arabs   are striking wondrous blows,
Lances are shattered,   and many burnished spears.

If you had been there   when shields were smashed to bits,
If you had heard   the hauberks meeting steel,
The sound of swords   grating on top of helms!
If you had seen   those valiant knights go down,
Screaming in anguish,   dying there on the ground—
Then you would know   what suffering can be!
This is a battle   heavy and hard to bear.
3490   The Emir prays,   asking Apollo's help,
Invokes Mohammed,   and Tervagant as well:
"Almighty gods,   I've served you faithfully,
You shall have idols   fashioned of purest gold! AOI
I ask you now   for triumph over Charles."
A trusted man,   Gemalfin, then comes forth
With woeful tidings   he gives to the Emir:
"Baligant, lord,   this is an evil day:
For you have lost   Malpramis, your fair son,
And Canabeus,   your brother, has been slain.
3500   Of the two Franks   who gained this victory,
I think that one   was Charlemagne himself,
For he was tall   and looked like a great lord,
His beard as white   as any April flower."
Then the Emir   sits with his head bent down,
Under the helmet   his face is stern and dark.
He feels he's dying,   so bitterly he grieves;
He calls Jangleu,   a man from overseas.

254

Says the Emir,   "Come forward now, Jangleu!
You have great courage,   and you are very wise;
3510   I've always found   your counsel to be true.
How do you see   the Arabs and the French?

3507. Jangleu d'Outremer
3510. Baligant's remark may mean that he has always followed Jangleu's
advice.

Are we to win   the honors of this field?"
Jangleu replies,   "Baligant, you are dead!
None of your gods   will ever save you now.
King Charles is fierce,   and valiant are the Franks—
I've never seen   such warlike men before.
But summon forth the Arabs,   lords of Occiant,
Turks, Enfruns, Giants,   to help you while they may.
Whatever happens,   there's no good in delay."

255

Outside his hauberk,   Baligant spreads his beard;   *3520*
The hawthorn flower   is not a purer white.
From what will come   he has no wish to hide.
Against his lips   he holds a clear-voiced horn,
And blows a call   which rings across the field;
The pagans, hearing,   rally their companies.
Those of Occiant   start to whinny and bray,
Men of Arguille   are barking like great dogs;
They charge the Franks   with overwhelming force,
Splitting their ranks;   the French give way, fall back,
And seven thousand   are killed in that attack.   *3530*

256

Ogier, no man   to do a craven deed—
As good a knight   as ever put on mail—
Sees the French ranks   broken and split apart.
He summons Thierry,   the Duke of the Argonne,
Count Jozeran   and Geoffroy of Anjou.
Then very fiercely   he speaks these words to Charles:

3526-7. This is not a pagan eccentricity, but the impression their languages
made on the Christians.

"See how the pagans   are killing off your men!
May God forbid   that your head wear a crown
If you won't fight   and so avenge your shame!"
3540   No one replies,   no one will speak a word;
Spurring their horses,   not to be left behind,
They charge to strike   whatever foes they find. AOI

257

Valiant in battle   are Charlemagne the King,
Naimon the Duke,   and Ogier the Dane,
Geoffroy of Anjou   who bore the flag for Charles.
There is a hero,   Count Ogier the Dane!
He spurs his horse   and gallops with all speed
To charge the pagan   who holds the Dragon high,
Strikes at Amborre   who crashes to the ground,
3550   With him the Dragon,   the ensign of the King.
Baligant sees   the standard-bearer fall,
Mohammed's banner,   dishonored, come to grief;
Then the Emir   begins to understand
That he is wrong,   and Charlemagne is right;
The Arab pagans   aren't making so much noise.
The Emperor Charles   calls out then to the Franks:
"Lords, will you help me?   I ask it in God's name."
The Franks reply,   "Why ask what you should know?
Cursed be the man   whose striking arm is slow!" AOI

258

3560   The day goes by;   darkness begins to fall;
Pagans and Franks   are fighting with their swords.
Two men of courage   command these mighty hosts.
They don't forget   to sound their battle-calls,
The great Emir   shouting his "Précieuse!"
And Charlemagne,   his famous cry "Montjoie!"

Each recognizes   the other's strong clear voice,
And then they meet   upon the battlefield.
They charge head on;   each one lands with his spear
So great a blow   upon the other's shield
It breaks wide open   below the heavy boss;   3570
The hauberk panels   are cracked and split apart,
And yet the spearheads   don't penetrate the flesh.
The girths give way,   throwing the saddles off,
With them, both Kings   come crashing to the ground.
Then, in an instant,   they have regained their feet
And drawn their swords,   ready to fight it out.
No way to end   this combat will be found
Till one of them   lies dead upon the ground. AOI

259

A mighty hero   is Charlemagne of France,
And Baligant   will meet him unafraid.   3580
With swords unsheathed,   they come together now,
Their heavy shields   receiving mighty blows
Which split the leathers,   the double wooden frames;
The nails fall out,   the bosses break apart.
Then nothing shelters   the hauberks from the blades,
And fiery sparks   come flashing from their helms.
This is a combat   which has to last as long
As neither man   admits that he is wrong. AOI

260

Says the Emir,   "Charles, if you stop and think,
You will repent   of what you've done to me: 3590
You can't deny   that you have killed my son;
You do great wrong   when you invade my lands.
Become my vassal,   hold them in fief to me;
Come and serve me,   from here to the Orient."

King Charles replies,   "That would be vile disgrace.
I'll be no friend   to pagans, or make peace.
Receive the law   that is the gift of God,
Become a Christian,   and you shall know my love;
Serve Him, have faith   in that almighty King."
3600   Says Baligant,   "Tediously you preach!"
They draw their swords,   and there's an end to speech.

261

The great Emir   is powerful and brave:
He strikes Charles' helmet   so terrible a blow
The burnished steel   is cracked and splits apart,
The sword blade cleaves   the Emperor's thick hair
And slices off   a hand's breadth of his scalp,
Stripping the flesh   down to the naked bone.
Charlemagne staggers,   comes close to falling down,
But God won't have him   brought to defeat or slain:
3610   Saint Gabriel   comes back to him once more,
And says, "Great King,   what are you waiting for?"

262

Charlemagne hears   the angel's holy voice:
He's not afraid,   he knows he will not die.
His strength returns,   his mind is clear and calm.
And then he strikes   with the great sword of France;
The Emir's helmet,   ablaze with jewels, cracks,
His head is broken   so that the brains spill out,
His face splits open   down to his long white beard:
He is stone dead   before he hits the ground.
3620   Then Charles' "Montjoie!"   rings through the battlefield.
Duke Naimon hears him   and hastens to his side
With Tencendur;   the great King mounts his horse.
Now by God's will,   the pagans turn and flee;
The Frenchmen know   they've won their victory.

263

The pagans flee,   for that is what God wills,
The Franks, with Charles,   are riding in pursuit.
The Emperor says,   "My lords, avenge your grief,
Relieve your anger   and you will cheer your hearts;
I saw this morning   how tears flowed from your eyes."
They answer, "Sire,   that is what we must do."   *3630*
So many pagans   the Franks cut down and slay
That very few   manage to get away.

264

The day is hot,   the air is thick with dust;
The pagans flee,   still harried by the Franks:
To Saragossa   they chase them all the way.
Queen Bramimonde   has gone up to her tower;
With her are clerics,   the priesthood of her faith,
That false religion   for which God has no love:
They're not ordained,   nor have they tonsured heads.
She sees the Arabs   running in wild retreat,   *3640*
And cries aloud,   "Mohammed, help us now!
Alas, fair King,   our men have fled the field,
The great Emir,   dishonored, has been slain!"
When Marsile hears her,   he turns to face the wall,
Tears fill his eyes,   he lets his head sink down;
He dies of grief   that nothing can console,
And to quick demons   yields up his sinful soul. AOI

265

Dead are the pagans,   except for those who fled,
And Charlemagne   is master of the field.
In Saragossa,   the gate is beaten down,   *3650*
There's no one left   who will defend it now.
Charles takes the stronghold;   his people come inside;

By right of conquest   they sleep there that same night.
Proud is the King   whose beard is silver-grey!
And Bramimonde   has yielded all the towers,
Ten that are large   and fifty that are small.
He does great things   who on God's aid can call!

266

The day is over;   now in the dark of night
The moon shines clear,   and stars flame in the sky.
3660   All Saragossa   belongs to Charlemagne.
A thousand Frenchmen   go searching through the town,
Through mosques and temples   of pagan infidels;
With iron hammers   and axes in their hands
They break the idols,   and all the images,
Putting an end   to magic sorcery.
The King loves God,   and wants to serve Him well;
Calling his bishops,   he has the water blessed,
And then the pagans   are brought to be baptized.
If there are any   who still resist King Charles,
3670   He has them hanged,   or killed by fire or sword.
A hundred thousand   and a good many more
Become true Christians;   only the Queen is left.
She will be taken,   a captive, to sweet France
To be converted   by love, as Charles commands.

267

Act II

The night has passed;   when the bright day appears,
Charles leaves a guard   in Saragossa's towers:
A thousand of his knights   remain behind
To hold the city   in the Emperor's name.
The King rides on   with all his other men
3680   And Bramimonde   he holds against her will—
But Charles desires   only to do her good.

In joy and triumph   the Frenchmen leave for home;
They seize Nerbone,   continue on their way,
And when they reach   Saint Scurin's in Bordeaux,
Charles stops to leave   upon the alter there
The Oliphant,   filled up with gold and coins,
As all the pilgrims   who pass that way can see.
Finding large boats,   for crossing the Gironde,
King Charles escorts   his nephew into Blaye,
And his companion,   the noble Oliver,   3690
And the Archbishop,   so valiant and so wise.
In white stone coffins   Charles has the three lords placed;
In Saint-Romain   the noble barons lie.
The Franks commend them   to God and to His names.
Charlemagne rides   through valleys, over hills—
He will not stop   until he reaches Aix;
There he draws rein   beside the mounting block.
From his high palace   the Emperor sends out
His messengers   to judges of his court.
Saxons, Bavarians,   Frisians, men of Lorraine,   3700
To Alemans   and men of Burgundy,
And Poitevins,   Normans and Bretons too,
Frenchmen whose wisdom   Charles can rely upon.
Soon will begin   the trial of Ganelon.

trial by ordeal — winner of fight is on God's side.
compurgation by (character) witness

268

The Emperor Charles   has now returned from Spain.
He comes to Aix,   his capital in France,
Enters the palace   and goes to the great hall.
Aude, a lovely maiden,   comes to him there.
She asks the King: "Where is the chieftain Count,

3694. There were prayers containing lists of the various names of God.
3708. There flows through Carcasonne in southwest France, a river called the Aude in memory of Roland's fiancée. I am grateful to Kathleen Micklow for this information.

3710   Roland, who swore   that I would be his wife?"
Charles, as she speaks,   is overcome with grief;
Tears fill his eyes,   he pulls at his white beard:
"Sister, sweet friend,   I can't bring back the dead.
But I will give you   a better match instead.
You'll marry Louis—   that's all that I can do—
He is my son,   and he shall rule my realm."
Aude replies,   "Your words seem to me strange.
The saints and angels,   almighty God forbid
That I live on   when Roland has been slain!"
3720   Her color fades,   she falls down at Charles' feet,
And dies—may God   have mercy on her soul!
The lords of France   mourn her and weep for woe.

269

Aude the fair   has taken leave of life.
Charlemagne thinks   that she has only swooned;
The Emperor feels   such pity that he weeps.
He takes her hands,   and draws her to her feet;
Upon her shoulder   her head hangs limply down.
Charles understands   that she is really dead.
He summons then   four noble countesses,
3730   Has Aude's body   borne to a nunnery;
There they keep vigil   all night until the dawn.
Beside the altar   she has an honored grave,
Richly endowed   by will of Charlemagne. AOI

270

The Emperor Charles   has come back home to Aix.
There Ganelon,   the traitor, bound with chains,
In the high town,   before the palace stands.
To a great stake   the serfs have bound him fast,
Both of his hands   are tied with deerskin thongs,
They beat him well   with heavy sticks and rods:

That way he's treated   in the most proper style,   *3740*
And he must wait   in torment for his trial.

271

As it is written   in the old chronicles,
Charlemagne summoned   vassals from many lands;
And in the chapel   at Aix they're gathered now.
The day is solemn,   the feast they celebrate
Is Saint Silvester's—   so many people say.
The trial begins   with speeches on both sides,
And Ganelon,   who did a traitor's deed,
Is dragged before   the Emperor to plead. AOI

272

"Barons, my lords,"   says Charlemagne the King,   *3750*
"Give me your judgment   concerning Ganelon.
He was with me in Spain,   among my host,
And there he robbed me   of twenty thousand Franks;
My nephew Roland   you'll never see again,
Nor Oliver,   so courteous and brave—
For gold and treasure   this man betrayed the Peers."
"Sire," says the Count,   "I won't conceal the truth:
Because of Roland   I lost both goods and gold.
I wanted him   to suffer and to die;
But in that vengeance   there was no treachery."   *3760*
The Franks reply,   "We'll talk of this and see."

273

Before the King,   behold Count Ganelon.
Stalwart he stands,   fair color in his face—
If he were loyal,   he'd look a noble lord.
He sees the French,   the judges who are there,

The thirty members   of his own family,
And then he speaks,   his great voice ringing out:
"Barons of France,   for God's sake hear me now!
My lords, I fought   beside the Emperor,
3770   And served him well   in loyalty and love.
His nephew Roland,   hating me in his heart,
Had me condemned   to torment and sure death:
I was to bring   Charles' message to Marsile—
I had the wit   and wisdom to survive.
I faced Count Roland   and challenged him aloud,
And Oliver,   and all the other Peers.
Charlemagne heard me,   so did these noble lords:
I am avenged,   but not by treachery."
The Franks reply,   "We'll go and judge your plea."

274

3780   Ganelon sees   his great trial has begun.
Thirty kinsmen   the Count has with him there,
Among them one   looked up to by the rest
Called Pinabel—   his castle is Sorence.
This man can argue   so that his views prevail,
And he's a hero   not easy to defeat. AOI
Ganelon says,   "In you, my friend . . .
Save me from death,   defend me in this trial!"
Says Pinabel,   "In no time you'll be free.
If any Frenchman   decides that you should hang,
3790   He must submit   to judgment on the field;
My good steel sword   will bring him to defeat!"
Count Ganelon   falls prostrate at his feet.

275

Bavarians, Saxons,   have gone to judge the case,
Normans are with them,   Poitevins, men of France,

it.
l,
end,
King

3800

ife.
w."

'. AOI

e,

efense."
ense."

3810

k,
e."
AOI

his trial;
much noise.
heard.
d fight."

g.

se,

fief, given now to the King,
vassal is killed. Similarly in

His hair is black,   his face is rather dark;
He isn't tall,   nor could you call him short.
With courtesy   he tells the Emperor:
"Fair Sire and King,   do not give way to grief!
You know I've served you   a long time faithfu
Now all my forebears   through me protest th
However Roland   may have wronged Ganelo
No one may harm   a man who serves the Kin
Count Ganelon   is thus a traitor proved;

3830   His oath to you   was broken and betrayed.
And so I judge   that he should hang and die
And that his body   be treated as . . .
A criminal   who's guilty of a crime.
If he has kinsmen   who'd argue this with m
I'll use this sword   girded here at my side
To give my judgment   a prompt and sure d
The Franks reply,   "Your argument makes s

278

Now Pinabel   stands up before the King;
He's tall and strong,   valiant and very swif

3840   The man he strikes   won't see another da
He says to Charles,   "Sire, you convoked
Pray, then, keep order—   let's not have s
And as for Thierry,   his judgment has bee
I say he's wrong—   now let him come an
His right-hand glove   he offers to the Kin
The Emperor says,   "I ask for hostages."
His thirty kinsmen   will sponsor Pinabel

glove, as in line 2838, symbolizes the
to whom it will revert in case the

Says Charlemagne,   "He's free then, in your place."
They will be guarded   till justice ends the case. AOI

279

When Thierry sees   that Pinabel will fight,   3850
He gives his glove,   the right one, to the King,
To return for hostages,   Charles sets him free.
Charles has four benches   arranged to mark the field;
Those who will fight   go out to take their seats.
All think the challenge   well given, rightly met;
Ogier explains   how they are to proceed.
Horses and arms   are sent for with all speed.

280

The knights are ready   to meet for their ordeal. AOI
They've made confession,   have been absolved and blessed,
They've heard a mass,   taken communion too;   3800
Great offerings   they've given to the church.
Now when the champions   appear before the King,
They both are wearing   sharp spurs upon their feet,
They've put on hauberks,   shining and light and strong,
Their burnished helmets   are closed around their heads,
They gird on swords   whose hilts are of pure gold.
Around their necks   they hang their quartered shields,
Their right hands grasp   the long sharp-pointed spears.
Now they have mounted   war-horses bred for speed.
Seeing them go,   a hundred thousand knights   3870
Remember Roland   and weep for Thierry—
For God knows what   the end of this will be!

3852. It is possible that Charles himself acted as hostage for Thierry.

281

In a broad meadow   below Aix la Chapelle,
The barons meet;   their battle has begun.
Both are courageous,   both of them valiant lords,
And their war-horses   are spirited and swift.
They spur them hard,   and loosening the reins,
They charge each other   and strike with all their might.
Both shields are shattered—   they're broken into bits—
3880   The hauberks break,   the girths are split apart,
The saddles fall,   and with them both the knights.
A hundred thousand   are weeping at the sight.

282

Both chevaliers   have fallen to the ground. AOI
Losing no time,   they're on their feet again.
Agile and swift   is Pinabel, and strong;
They face each other—   they have no horses now—
And raise their swords,   whose hilts are made of gold,
To strike and hew   each other's shining helms;
Those heavy blows   can cut right through the steel.
3890   The French lament,   thinking their man must fail.
"O God," says Charles,   "now let the right prevail!"

283

Says Pinabel,   "Thierry, admit you've lost!
I'll be your vassal   in loyalty and love,
All I possess   shall be at your command—
But reconcile   the King and Ganelon."
Then Thierry answers,   "That's easy to decide!

I'll take no offer   unworthy of a knight!
Let God determine   which one of us is right!" AOI

284

And Thierry says,   "Pinabel, you are brave;
You're tall and strong,   your body is well built,   *3900*
That you are valiant   is known to all your peers.
You can afford   to let this battle go!
I'll make your peace   with Charlemagne the King,
But Ganelon   must get what he deserves—
No day will pass   without his death retold."
Says Pinabel,   "Almighty God forbid!"
I stand here now   for all my family—
I won't surrender   to any man on earth!
Better to die   than live to merit blame."
So once again   they slash with their great swords,   *3910*
Striking the helmets   brilliant with gold and jewels—
Great fiery sparks   fly out against the sky.
Now neither champion   will to the other yield
Until a dead man   is lying on the field. AOI

285

He's a strong fighter,   Pinabel of Sorence,
The blow he strikes   on Thierry's burnished helm
Sends out such sparks   the grass is set on fire.
Then he springs forward,   the point of his steel blade
Cutting right through   from Thierry's forehead down;
Along his face   the sword point slashes deep,   *3920*
And blood spring out   all over his right cheek;
Down to his waist   the hauberk is all red—
Without God's help,   no doubt he would be dead! AOI

286

When Thierry sees   he's wounded in the face,
His bright blood falling   over the meadow grass,
Pinabel's helmet   of burnished steel he strikes:
Down through the nose-piece   it cracks and splits in two,
His skull is broken   and spills the brains inside;
With one last flourish   Thierry has felled him dead—
3930 With that great blow   he's master of the field.
The Frenchmen shout,   "A holy miracle!
Justice demands   that Ganelon must die,
With all the kinsmen   who came and took his side." AOI

287

Thierry has won   his triumph on the field.
The Emperor Charles   comes out to give him thanks;
Accompanied   by forty noble lords,
Among them Naimon,   Count Ogier the Dane,
William of Blaye   and Geoffroy of Anjou.
King Charlemagne   takes Thierry in his arms,
3940 And wipes his face   with royal marten furs;
These he puts down—   they bring another cloak.
Thierry's armor   is gently taken off,
And he is mounted   on an Arabian mule.
Most joyfully   they bring the hero home;
They come to Aix   and in the square dismount.
Now they will kill   the kinsmen of the Count.

288

Charlemagne summons   the nobles of his court:
"What do you counsel   about my hostages?
These men came here   to plead for Ganelon,
3950 And stayed as pledges,   sponsoring Pinabel."

The Franks reply,   "Ill work if one survives!"
The King commands   an officer, Basbrun:
"Go hang them all   upon the gallows tree!
And by my beard   whose hair is silver-grey,
If one escapes,   you're dead and put to shame."
The man replies,   "I'll do as you command."
A hundred servants   help him to drag them off;
They hang all thirty   that they were told to take.
So one man's evil   draws others in its wake. AOI

289

They all agree: Bavarians, Alemans,   *3960*
Poitevins, Bretons,   and men from Normandy,
And first of all   the Franks who come from France,
That Ganelon   should die most horribly.
And so they order   four war-horses brought out
To which they tie   Ganelon's feet and hands.
These are proud chargers,   spirited, bred for speed:
Four servants urge them   the way they are to go.
There where a river   across a meadow flows,
Count Ganelon   is utterly destroyed:
His ligaments   are twisted and stretched out,   *3970*
His every limb   is cracked and splits apart;
On the green grass   the bright blood runs in streams.
So Ganelon   as a foul traitor died.
Let no man's treason   give comfort to his pride!

290

The Emperor Charles,   his vengeance being done,
Summoned his bishops,   the ones who came from France,
Bavarians   and Alemans as well:
"A noble captive   is dwelling in my house;
She's heard such sermons   and edifying tales,

3980 She trusts in God,   and wants to take the Faith.
      Baptize her now,   that God may have her soul."
      The bishops answer,   "Let godmothers be found!"
      ...   ...high-born ladies."
      A great assembly   was gathered at the baths
      To see the Queen of Spain   receive the Faith;
      To Juliana   they now have changed her name.
      She had true knowledge   when Christian she became.

291

      The Emperor Charles,   once justice has been done,
3990 And his great anger   is finally appeased,
      Has Bramimonde   baptized into the Faith.
      The day is over,   and in the dark of night
      The King lies sleeping   in his high vaulted room.
      Saint Gabriel   is sent by God to say:
      "Charlemagne, summon   your Empire's mighty hosts!
      You'll march in force   into the land of Bire;
      You must relieve   King Vivien at Imphe
      Where pagans hold   his city under siege,
      And Christian voices   are crying for your help."
      The Emperor Charles   has no desire to go.
4000 "God!" says the King,   "how weary is my life!"
      He pulls his beard,   the tears flow from his eyes.
      Here ends the poem,   for Turoldus declines.

4002. The ending of the poem, *Ci falt la geste que Turoldus declinet,* is very famous for being so enigmatic. *Que* may mean either "which" or "because" (Jenkins); *declinet* may mean "to compose, sing, recite, or copy." It may also mean "to set," as the sun sets, or "to become infirm." I hoped mainly to let the poem end with the same frustrating vagueness as does the original.